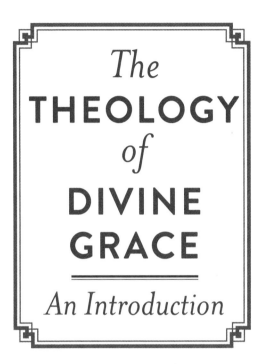

The
THEOLOGY
of
DIVINE
GRACE

An Introduction

JOSEPH THOMAS

Scepter

Published by Scepter Publishers, Inc.
info@scepterpublishers.org
www.scepterpublishers.org
800-322-8773
New York

Cover Image: *Divine Grace* (2011) by Patricia Brintle, acrylic on canvas, private collection, photo credit © Patricia Brintle
Cover Design: Studio Red Design
Page Design: Rose Design

Library of Congress Control Number: 2023901111

ISBN paperback: 9781594174803
ISBN eBook: 9781594174810

Printed in the United States of America

Contents

Introduction

JESUS CHRIST "FULLY REVEALS MAN TO MAN HIMSELF." Nearly sixty years ago, the Second Vatican Council proclaimed this truth, which still has such resonance for us today. These words remind us that only Christ offers the definitive truth about human nature.

Many people today ask: What is the meaning of the human being and his existence? Some deny the very reality of human nature. Others reduce the human person to certain material or psychological elements.

The area of theology known as *theological anthropology* studies the profound truths revealed by God regarding the meaning of the human person, created in God's image and called to communion with the Trinity and with the rest of humanity.

An important step in God's plan for us is the gift of *grace*, by which we come to participate in God's own life. This book seeks to examine various aspects of the mystery of grace and its action in the person.

God's entry into our life does not take away from our own dignity, as many people today fear. Rather, God always respects our freedom while he also leads us to a new and exalted grandeur, that of being a son of God. As St. John Paul II noted, the man who enters into the mystery of Christ, even with the awareness of "his weakness and sinfulness," comes to a new-found adoration of God but also a "deep wonder at himself." We can resolve to approach the mystery of grace's action in man with this sense of awe, accompanied by reason and faith, so that we might also proclaim this truth to our world today.

CHAPTER 1

Man's Calling to Communion with God

Man's Ultimate Purpose:
To Participate in the Inner Life of God

Many people today realize that, deep down, each person has a profound longing that can only be satisfied by God. God's revelation answers this longing in a way which we could never have imagined. Scripture shows us that not only are we called to adore God, but we are called to participate in the very inner life of the divinity, Father, Son, and Holy Spirit.

God has created man with this final goal in mind. It is in light of this call to communion with the Trinity, as the Second Vatican Council stated, that the human person has been created with such lofty dignity: "The root reason for human dignity lies in man's call to communion with God."

We naturally tend to think that our own existence as creatures comes before our relationship with God. In the order of time, this is indeed the case. But from God's point of view, his call to raise us to the divine life comes before our very existence. Our existence is oriented toward communion with God and receives its full meaning precisely in this communion. As the Council went on to note, "Man would not exist were he not created by God's love and constantly preserved by it; and he cannot live fully according to truth unless he freely acknowledges that love and devotes himself to His Creator."

Because this special call to communion with God determines man's identity, the human person can never be fully satisfied with goals that fall short of God himself. We can appreciate this longing in the two spiritual capacities present in the person: the *intellect* and the *will*. Both of these powers tend toward the infinite. Our mind seeks an ever greater and more perfect truth; our will seeks the ultimate good which goes beyond all limited goods.

The great thirteenth-century Dominican St. Thomas Aquinas observed that the reality of the human intellect shows our natural desire for God. Aquinas makes reference to a phenomenon well known to our experience: our natural desire to know the "why" behind things. We human beings have a desire to know exactly why and how the world came into being. Such a desire, as the Dominican notes, gives rise to *wonder* at the world around us. We can think, for example, of the multitude of questions a child might ask her parents: Why does the sun come up in the morning? Why do the leaves fall off the tree when it gets cold? And so on.

These questions, Aquinas observes, can never simply be answered in partial ways. Our intellect has a longing for not just part of the truth but the entire truth. We want to know the fundamental cause of everything that exists and what the purpose of everything is. In the final analysis, our desire to know about the world around us can only fully be satisfied in God. Otherwise, if nothing can fully satisfy the quests of the human intellect, our natural desire for the truth would be frustrated. Yet it wouldn't make sense for us to have desires if those desires couldn't be fulfilled in some way.

This same pattern of thought can help us to appreciate why the will also has a natural longing for God. The will is that power of our human soul which moves us to desire the good that we grasp in our mind. The will is that capacity, for example, which might lead us to eat ice cream when our senses feel attracted to that item of food. In that case, our will seeks out that enjoyment with the desire that this treat will lead us to fulfillment.

Certainly, we might find satisfaction in that cup of ice cream. But this would only be true to a limited degree. The enjoyment which comes from that experience would soon wear off. Our will naturally tends toward much higher goods. The human will seeks something much greater than the limited human goods of this earth. The German theologian Jutta Burggraf pointed out that our will, "by its very nature . . . tends to transcend itself; it is directed at something beyond, toward the infinite." Like the intellect, the will seeks for that fullness of good which can only be found in God.

Therefore, in the very core of our being we possess longings for truth and goodness which also manifest our desire for God. However, it is also important to keep in mind that the mere presence of these longings does not necessarily lead to their fulfillment. While it's not easy for us to admit our dependence on God, our human nature stands in absolute need of God's help to reach its true end. Only by the gratuitous gift of God, who has chosen to reveal himself through Christ and in the Holy Spirit, can we fully enter into the knowledge and love of God. The free gift of God's grace is necessary so that we might reach that end for which we were created.

God, from all eternity, has wanted man to share in his own divine life. Through this will of God, we can realize the purpose for which we were created. While this plan has existed from all eternity, it is carried out in the reality of *time* and *history*. The very existence of time reminds us that created things are in a state of constant change and movement. The human person, in particular, is subject to changes of one type or another, due to the changeableness of the material world as well as our own free choices.

God's decision to reveal himself to us gives a new meaning to this temporal dimension. The ancients tended to see time in terms of alternating phases of growth and decay, which would go on endlessly in a cyclical manner. God's revelation to his Chosen People reveals to us that time has a beginning, in the act of Creation, and also an end which God has in mind. As a result, time and history take on a new meaning. Time becomes a domain in which the human being can respond to God's invitation to communion with him.

The revelation in Jesus Christ takes up this Old Testament sense of time, as the dimension in which God's saving action takes place. The New Testament shows us that the definitive salvation of God, foretold by the Old Testament, has indeed taken place in history in the incarnate Son of God. Christ begins his public ministry announcing that "the time is fulfilled, and the kingdom of God is at hand; repent, and believe in the gospel" (Mk 1:15). The Gospel text uses the word *kairos* to indicate time. Time is no longer *chronos*, the more general word for time, which refers to simply a succession of moments. Rather, time is *kairos*, a word which indicates the "right time" or a particularly suitable moment of time.

In light of God's definitive entrance into history through the Word made flesh, time has become more than simply an endless cycle of change, as many ancients thought. Time has become a dimension through which man, who exists in history, can enter into contact with the eternal divine life. We are therefore called to appreciate our existence in time as the special and limited period that God offers us to respond to his offer of friendship and thus realize the ultimate purpose for which he has created us. Josemaría Escrivá, the twentieth-century

Spanish saint and tireless preacher of the universal call to holiness, observed that we are called to live in the conviction that "we mustn't squander this period of the world's history which God has entrusted to each one of us."

The Natural and Supernatural Orders

Everything which is good comes from God, whether it is a beautiful tree or the gift of redemption offered through the sacrament of baptism. These two goods are of very different types and orders, and in keeping with this fact theology has traditionally distinguished between two levels of reality: the *natural* and the *supernatural*.

The word *natural*, or *nature*, can have various meanings depending on the context. The word originally comes from the Latin term *natura*, which comes from *nasci*, meaning "to be born." In keeping with this etymology, our "nature" is what we have from our birth. More broadly, nature is the specific makeup that a certain thing has. We could speak of human nature, of the nature of a plant or animal, or of nature as indicating everything created by God. In each of these cases, that which has a "nature" has a certain completeness to it. Nature has been created by God and is ordered to God, but it has its own existence outside of God.

It is important to value nature in itself but also to see it within its greater context. Nature has its own being but is ordered to something greater, which goes beyond nature, and which we call the *supernatural*. It is not always easy to distinguish between the two levels, and the relationship between the natural and supernatural orders has been the source of intense debate among theologians for the last century. In the case of human beings, as we have considered, we are beings with a spiritual soul, united to our body, and we find our fulfillment precisely in communion with God. Still, theology has traditionally distinguished between what we can do by nature (things we can do on our own) and what we can do by God's supernatural gift (things we can only do with God's help).

We can all recognize that there are certain things we can do with the strength of the nature that God has given us from birth. We can generally carry out certain activities such as walking, eating, and reading, and we don't necessarily need extra help from God to do so. We can even know and love God, to a limited extent, with the capacity of our human nature.

Nonetheless, God has created us for a destiny that goes far beyond these natural capacities, however valuable they might be. He has called us to enter into a personal relationship of knowledge and love with the Blessed Trinity itself, and for this we are in need of the supernatural gift of grace. Our nature needs to receive a new kind of nature, which is the supernatural.

The supernatural level of existence does not take away our nature but raises it to a radically new level in which we can live as sons of God. As the nineteenth-century German theologian Matthias Joseph Scheeben stated, the gift of supernatural life involves "a transfiguration and elevation of our whole nature with all its faculties to a higher sphere." The gift of grace gives the person a new strength by which his mind, his will, and his whole being can enter in that full communion with God for which he was created.

Sacred Scripture uses a series of terms that evoke the important distinction between the natural and the supernatural order. St. Paul describes the Christian, raised to the level of divine life by baptism, as a "new creation" (2 Cor 5:17). Christ, risen from the dead, is the source of divine life through which the entire human race can be created anew. Grace allows for the creation of a new human race, freed from the bonds of sin and capable of living in friendship with God.

As Christians, we could say we are fond of the word *new*: in addition to the "new creation," we speak of the "New Testament," which contains the full revelation of God in Christ, as well as the *new covenant*, which brings to fullness the *old covenant* between God and the Chosen People of the Old Testament. In light of the teaching of St. Paul and the Fathers of the Church, the Church recognizes Christ as the New Adam.

We might ask: What exactly is the relationship between the "new" and the "old" in this scriptural perspective? It's evident to us that the "new," in the case of Christ, is superior to the old. Paul speaks of the "old self" in relation to the "sinful body" (Rom 6:6). The apostle also speaks of the "old covenant" as indicating a fleeting glory, in contrast to the glory of Christ as revealed in the new covenant (2 Cor 3:7–18). The law of the old covenant serves to show the reality of man's sin, since without faith in Christ man is unable to hold to God's commandment (Rom 3:19–20).

However, this special value of the "new," in relation to Christ, should not lead us to dismiss the "old." The old order, that of the state of creation before Christ, is certainly marked by sin. But this old order is also a first step toward the fulfillment of creation that would come about in Christ. So, while in the Letter to the Romans Paul reminds us that Adam's sin has brought a state of guilt for all (5:18), in the First Letter to the Corinthians the apostle also sees Adam as the initial stage that leads to Christ: "Thus it is written, 'The first man Adam became a living being'; the last Adam a life-giving spirit." The "spiritual," the Apostle of the Gentiles concludes, comes after the "physical" (meaning "natural") (1 Cor 15:45–46).

These images from Scripture can help us to appreciate that which is "new," or the supernatural elevation of the person through Christ, while at the same time to recognize the intrinsic value of what is "old," or what human nature possessed before the coming of Christ. In a similar way, our effort to appreciate what is supernatural should not lead us to dismiss that which is natural.

In examining these two terms, the *natural* and the *supernatural*, the Church has had to strike a delicate balance between different perspectives, which we will examine later in this book. In the early centuries, the Church faced Pelagianism, a way of thinking that has always had a certain appeal, even to our own day. This view held that man's nature has within itself the origin of the good, including that supernatural good for which it was created. Later, there emerged the other extreme, held by the Lutherans in the sixteenth century and the Jansenists in the seventeenth and eighteenth centuries. This position held that man's nature was completely damaged by original sin, to the point that he has lost even the most remote capacity for good.

In the face of these different ways of understanding man in his present condition, the terms *natural* and *supernatural* have been an important way by which the Church has expressed the present condition of man and his need for grace. The human being, wounded by sin, has lost his capacity to reach his supernatural end, but he is still capable of acting in another realm, which is the natural. The natural order reminds us of the dignity that God has given to human nature, and which this nature, albeit wounded by sin, continues to possess. The supernatural order reminds us that our human nature is in need of help from God to reach its fulfillment.

In keeping with this perspective, an opinion of some theologians who interpret the work of Thomas Aquinas has been to appreciate that human nature has its own particular end. This natural end is different from the goal that is made possible by grace. The important sixteenth-century commentator on Aquinas, Thomas de Vio Caetano, or Cajetan, defended the position that the supernatural order is a gratuitous gift of God. Cajetan insisted that supernatural life remains beyond the natural desire of the person. He went to the extreme of saying, contrary to Aquinas, that the beatific vision is not the fulfillment of our desires, but only the end of grace. That is, we can desire the perfect vision of God only because God gives us a special grace to do so. From this point of view, it became common to speak of a "pure human nature," which has its own specific end separate from the immediate vision of God in heaven, or the beatific vision.

The notion of a "pure human nature," while it is a theological idea and not part of the Church's teaching, serves to emphasize that human nature can be studied as a reality unto itself, separate from God's decision to raise this nature to the divine life through grace. This idea helps us to appreciate the distinction between the natural and the supernatural. Still, we also need to be careful about creating too much of a separation between the natural and the supernatural. Cajetan's thought can lead us to see our supernatural end as something that is externally "added on" to our human nature. Our human nature, according to his view, does not by itself long for the beatific vision.

Aquinas does indeed hold, following Aristotle, that we can distinguish a natural end to human nature, which the human being can attain with his own natural powers. This natural end consists in the contemplation of God, insofar as the human intellect can accomplish this with its own powers. However, this natural end goes along with the truth that our fullest end, or the complete happiness that we were made for, is to be found in the direct vision of God. This end, in the deepest sense, is utterly beyond the reach of our natural capacities.

So, while we can appreciate the specific good that man can attain with his own natural powers, such a recognition should also lead us to appreciate—as Aquinas affirms in his great work, the *Summa Theologiae*—that the ultimate end of man's nature is the perfect vision of God, only accessible with the help of God. Here, we face a paradox regarding our own nature: we have been created with a natural desire that our own nature cannot satisfy on its own. God created this nature in expectation of that fulfillment which God himself would provide through the gratuitous gift of grace.

Many theologians in more recent times, particularly the twentieth-century French theologian Henri de Lubac, have opposed the attempt to distinguish between a "natural" and a "supernatural" end of human nature. De Lubac—we note again that we are before a theological opinion, and not the teaching of the Church—rejected the idea of "pure nature" and stressed that man's nature is specifically ordered to the gift of grace that God has desired to grant him.

Such a perspective has the advantage of helping us to see how grace responds to the deepest desires of our very created being. However, it also runs the risk of making it more difficult to appreciate the specific value of human nature as a distinct reality from the supernatural order. Pope Pius XII cautioned against an excessive emphasis on the ordering of man to the divine life, which would lead us to think that God would somehow "need" to create intellectual beings who are called to the beatific vision. To posit such necessity on the part of God, he noted in the encyclical *Humani Generis* (1950), would prevent us from appreciating that salvation is a gratuitous gift, which God is in no way obliged to give us.

Our modern society, with its emphasis on the dignity and value of the individual, can sometimes make it difficult for us to appreciate our dependence on God for the gift of salvation. We might prefer to think that man, with the great dignity that he has from being created in God's image, is able to reach God through his own natural desires, or that God would be obliged to respond to our desire for him.

In summary, the Church has seen the need to distinguish between the natural and supernatural orders in man, even though these two orders are also intimately related to one another. Human nature, though it has a specific dignity even after sin, can only find its true fulfillment in God. As Vatican II's constitution *Gaudium et Spes* notes, "The ultimate vocation of man is in fact one, and divine." It is only through the grace which comes from *outside* of man that the inner being of man can be fully realized. As we have noted, an adequate understanding of the realities of the natural and supernatural orders requires a delicate balance, which involves always keeping in mind the distinction as well as the intimate relationship between these levels. In this way, we can appreciate the great goodness of human nature and at the same time be aware of its radical dependence on God, the fullness of good.

The Incarnation of the Word Sheds Light on Man and History

The ultimate harmony between the natural and the supernatural, at times so challenging for us to comprehend, is revealed though Jesus Christ. As we have seen, the Second Vatican Council taught that only in the mystery of the Incarnate Word does the mystery of man become clear. Later in the same document, *Gaudium et Spes*, the Church expressed the same reality in more detail: "The Lord is the goal of human history, the focal point of the longings of history and of civilization, the center of the human race, the joy of every heart and the answer to all its yearnings." This fullness of revelation in Christ offers to us that light which he stands in need of, not only about those things that go beyond our understanding, but also, as the First Vatican Council had noted, so that we may know truths that can be known by the power of human reason. In this way, as this Council commented, these latter truths can "be known readily by all with firm certitude and with no admixture of error," even in our present condition marked by sin.

The incarnation of Christ, then, is the definitive light offered by God that allows us to comprehend the full meaning of man and of history. When we think of light, we naturally think of that visible light which allows us to grasp the dimensions and features of the world around us: the sun, the sky, other persons, material objects. The presence of light allows us to see these objects around us in their perspective: how big something is, how far away it is, how its nature compares to other objects, and so forth. In a similar way, Christ, who is the "light of the world" (Jn 8:12), allows us to appreciate human nature and the created world within their truest perspective, which is that of God.

From the earliest centuries, the Church has had to staunchly defend the truth that Christ really did have a true human nature, separate from his divine nature as the Second Person of the Trinity. In the moment of the Incarnation, Christ took on a human nature while at the same time remaining the eternal Son of the Father. The human nature of Christ, while still having many of the limitations present in the current state of human nature, became filled with the divine life. In consequence, Jesus' human nature offers a vivid manifestation of the divine life. Yet Christ's human nature cannot fully reveal the divine nature, because the divine nature will always go beyond the limits of what is human.

Still, even with those limitations which are part and parcel of human nature, Christ in his humanity is "the image of the invisible God, the first-born of all creation" (Col 1:15). With these words, Paul indicates that Christ reflects and makes present God, but also shows the fullness of God's plan for human nature and all creation. John recounts our Lord's words from the Last Supper, which further remind us that Christ's human nature manifests the eternal mystery of God: "He who has seen me has seen the Father" (Jn 14:9).

So, in the midst of the various challenges we encounter in trying to understand the natural and supernatural orders, we can look to the mystery of Jesus Christ's true humanity as a reference point. Christ shows us, in the fullest sense, what it means for man to be in the image of God. He shows us that all aspects of human life can be an authentic reflection of the life of God. Through Christ, all the circumstances of human life—work, study, social relations, and even suffering—can be a way of living in communion with God. As *Gaudium et Spes* points out, in continuity with the Church's tradition, "[Christ] blazed a trail, and if we follow it, life and death are made holy and take on a new meaning." Our human nature, freed from the corruption of sin, can be raised to its supernatural fulfillment, but without losing its specific value as a created nature. In fact, precisely by the gift of supernatural grace, the true beauty of human nature can shine forth in its greatest splendor.

Predestination and the Vocation of Man

Predestination is a term often associated with the sixteenth-century Protestant reformer John Calvin. We will have the occasion to examine his thought in chapter nine. In the Bible, the word only appears in the New Testament and has the meaning of "to determine ahead of time" or "to set a limit ahead of time."

With the deep awareness that we have today of human freedom, we can naturally resist the idea that our lives are predestined. Certainly, if we did not appreciate the reality of our freedom, we would be missing an essential part of the Christian view of the person. Nonetheless, God's revelation also shows us that God's knowledge and plan always come before any action on our part. Referring to Christians, Paul tells us that "those whom he foreknew he also predestined to be conformed to the image of his Son" (Rom 8:29).

Predestination, from an authentically Christian point of view, refers to this divine plan, present before Creation, by which God desires to share his divine life with humanity. It is not a "destiny" given to the person, in the sense of a fate to which that person is predetermined. Predestination does not mean that we cannot act one way or the other, or that we cannot make specific choices among the various options available to us. Rather, predestination refers to God's choice to make human beings into adopted sons and daughters through Christ.

In the first place, this election regards Christ. God has chosen Christians "in him [Christ] before the foundation of the world" (Eph 1:4). In the deepest sense, it is Christ who has been chosen by the Father to be the source of salvation and holiness for the entire human race. God's special choice toward Christians is always in and through Christ.

In examining this theme, it is important to keep in mind the limits of language. Through the language of choice and predestination, Scripture seeks to express the mystery of God's love and initiative. In light of this truth, Christians are described as "elect" (Lk 18:7). Still, this does not mean that others are not the object of God's special love. In fact, God chooses particular persons, and a specific people, the Chosen People, precisely so that his love and salvation might reach everyone.

The reality of God's special choice gives rise to the Christian understanding of life as a *vocation* or calling. In ancient Greek, the verb "to call" could signify "to invite to a banquet" or "to summon." These meanings help to express the significance of that special choice which God has made to men in Christ, from all eternity. The Christian life proceeds from the awareness that God has personally invited us to an intimate sharing of life. Not just to Simon Peter but to all whom he has chosen, God gives a new name, which indicates that new identity which we receive as a fruit of God's special choice (Jn 1:42, Rv 2:17).

However, while the call of God is always the primary element in vocation, the concept of vocation also necessarily implies a human response. The French New Testament scholar Fernand Prat (d. 1938) noted that the word *called* generally refers to one who has not only heard the divine call, but also accepted it. A vocation implies that a person has both recognized God's special favor and also responded freely to this call.

With this interplay of God's action and our freedom, the reality of vocation takes shape in our life. At times, God's call gives rise to a specific divine vocation in a particular institution within the Church. Through that specific vocation, God grants us a special light to recognize the way in which we are called to live the Christian vocation to holiness, as well as a new strength so as to fulfill that specific mission in the service of the whole Church. Such a specific vocation is thus a very special manifestation of the reality of grace: God grants a vocation through his grace, allows us to live that vocation by his grace, and the vocation is oriented to a sharing in the divine life through grace. Such specific vocations, while not for everyone, manifest the special love and predilection which God has for each and every person.

God's decision to raise man to the supernatural order is a fulfillment of our human nature, but does not take away that nature. The divine initiative to re-establish intimacy with man, John Paul II noted, is a free action of God, but at the same time "has the surprising capacity to take man at the root, to respond to his aspiration for the infinite, to satisfy his thirst for being, for good, for truth and beauty which makes him restless."

This is an important point for the culture in which we live. Many people fear that a vocation would be an infringement upon their freedom, as if God's call would get in the way of their desire to realize their fulfillment as human beings. Nothing could be further from the truth. God's call brings our human capacities to their most profound realization. God raises our being to a participation in the divine life, while at the same time bringing out the deepest meaning of our noble aspirations as humans.

Within this perspective, we can better understand why Josemaría Escrivá proclaimed to Christians that "your human vocation is a part—and an important part—of your divine vocation." Through Christ, God wants all that is part of our human nature to be ordered to his glory. As the founder of Opus Dei went on to comment,

> That is the reason why you must strive for holiness, giving
> a particular character to your human personality, a style to

your life; contributing at the same time to the sanctification of others, your fellow men; sanctifying your work and your environment: the profession or job that fills your day, your home and family and the country where you were born and which you love.

By striving to attain this ideal, with the help of grace, Christians show forth in their lives the profound complementarity of the natural and the supernatural.

CHAPTER 2

The Meaning of Grace

Overview of the Term *Grace*

We are probably pretty familiar with the term *grace*. We recognize that this word expresses a key aspect of the Christian life. As the well-known American hymn exclaims: "Amazing grace! How sweet the sound / That saved a wretch like me." The song expresses the profound new reality experienced by those who believe: "I once was lost, but now am found, / Was blind, but now I see."

But what exactly is grace? Grace cannot be fully expressed by any one, single definition, because the word is an attempt to express the immense mystery of God's action to allow us to participate in his own divine life. In the broadest sense, as the Spanish theologian Juan Luis Lorda notes, the Christian tradition uses the term *grace* to describe all the gifts of salvation which God grants to us, so as to raise us from sin and lead us to our supernatural end. Along with this more general sense, *grace* can also be used in more specific senses, to express the particular forms that God's action in us can take.

The word *grace* is the English translation of the Greek word *charis*, which appears with frequency in the New Testament. It was not a specifically religious term. The word could refer to "that which delights" or "that which pleases." This sense was related to another meaning, which is that of a favor offered by one person, perhaps a god or a master, and received by another. Given that grace could involve both the act of giving and that of receiving, we can understand why the word was also associated with thanksgiving.

This linguistic context can help us to app damental aspect of grace. Grace is not a *thing* some kind of substance which God gives to us. involves a *relationship* of intimacy with God. Tl we are allowed to enter into the mystery of Gc and address him as Father, through the Son, and of the Holy Spirit.

Catholic theology makes use of the term *grac* view of this possibility, offered by God to man, of *participating* in the mystery of God. That is why it is not enough to simply use terms like *God* or *God's love* in place of *grace*. God always remains transcendent, but grace always implies a specific relationship between God and man. Through this relationship, human nature itself is raised to a higher and supernatural plane. So, grace is not simply an action of God, but the action by which God transforms us and leads us to a new and higher level of being, that of a son or daughter of God.

In this chapter we will examine the way Sacred Scripture describes this mysterious reality, as well as some key aspects of grace.

Grace in the Old Testament

The word *grace* or Greek *charis* corresponds to the Hebrew word *hen* in the Septuagint, the important ancient translation of the Hebrew Old Testament into Greek. As the twentieth-century Swiss biblical scholar Walther Zimmerli points out, the root word for *hen* describes "the kind turning of one person to another as expressed in an act of assistance." The word implies not simply a kind disposition, but rather an action through which this benevolent disposition is put into practice. While the Bible sometimes uses this word to characterize the kind actions of human beings toward one another, most of the time the term is used to portray God's action toward man. The psalmist makes use of a form of this word when he exclaims, "Be gracious to me, O Lord!" (Ps 9:13). The Old Testament is filled with the assurance of God's action in the face of man's dire need for it. While the People of God ask for God's help, they also recognize that God's loving kindness is always a gratuitous gift. As God exclaims to Moses, "I will be gracious to whom I will be gracious, and will show mercy on whom I will show mercy" (Ex 33:19).

The solemn proclamation of Yahweh's name, which occurs when God renews the covenant at Mount Sinai, offers one of the most profound Old Testament insights into the nature of grace: "The Lord passed before [Moses], and proclaimed, 'The Lord, the Lord, a God merciful and gracious, slow to anger, and abounding in steadfast love and faithfulness'" (Ex 34:6). Significantly, this revelation occurs after the People of Israel have defiled the original covenant at Mount Sinai by worshipping the golden calf. It is precisely at this moment that God reveals himself, for the first time in the Scriptures, as a God full of mercy and tenderness.

The Hebrew word *rahum*, meaning "merciful," is first used to describe Yahweh. The word indicates in a striking way God's compassion toward man. This word has the original sense of a physical feeling or an emotion. This is the sentiment which leads family members to feel a sense of oneness with each other, especially between parents and their children or between siblings. Jewish thought held that this feeling of compassion had its basis in the maternal bosom or the innermost part of the father's being.

While the original context of the word is physical, the word came to indicate something more spiritual: the attitude of freely given charity that God himself feels toward man. God is revealed to the Chosen People as a God filled with the immense love that a father or mother feels toward their child. In light of the reality of man's unfaithfulness to his covenant with God, the term would come to express God's pardoning grace in the face of sin, or mercy as we understand it today.

This description of God's mercy offers the fitting context for the description of God as "gracious," reflecting the Hebrew word for grace, *hen*. In the Old Testament, this word expresses not only the graciousness of God's love but also the way in which God's favor becomes a gift that remains within man. For example, Noah finds "favor" (*hen*) in the eyes of God, as does Moses (Gn 6:8; Ex 33:12). In a mysterious way, man comes to share in the favor that God bestows freely. This gift of grace is even associated with a beauty that God gives to man (Ps 45:2). Even in the Old Testament, the revelation of God's compassion reveals to us his desire to fill us with the special gift of his favor. The power of grace is shown not simply in the revelation of God's love, but also in that fact that this love lifts us to a higher level of existence.

The text of Exodus 34 goes on to describe God as "abounding in steadfast love." This phrase makes use of another Hebrew word, *hesed*, which also has a deep resonance in Scripture. The original context of the word refers not simply to God, but to a helpful act which is part of a relationship of trust. Such an act might be expected as part of a mutual relationship, in which a friend expects the help of a friend. Applied to God, the word came to take on a special meaning. It would refer to the faithful and merciful help the People of God expect because of the covenant God has made with them. In this context, *hesed* is a particularly meaningful word for understanding the nature of grace. The term expresses the free and gratuitous help that God grants to man, but it also reminds us that this help is part of an ongoing covenant or relationship.

The final word used to describe Yahweh in this passage from Exodus is the Hebrew word *emet*, meaning "truth" or "faithfulness." In the Old Testament perspective, truth is not simply a philosophical concept but also has a strong moral dimension. God's truthfulness expresses his faithfulness to his word and is therefore closely connected to *hesed*. As the psalmist says, addressing God, "Steadfast love (*hesed*) and faithfulness (*emet*) go before thee" (Ps 89:14). God is preeminently faithful in his actions and commitments, and for this reason the People of God can place their trust in him.

From the Old Testament perspective, then, we can understand grace as the loving attitude of God who, freely and without any merit on our part, comes to the aid of his people. This benevolence is shown first of all in the very act of Creation, in which God, "in a plan of sheer goodness freely created man to make him share in his own blessed life."

But God's benevolence is particularly manifested in his choice of the people of Israel. Such election was special but not exclusive. The Chosen People understood that through God's special love for them, all of humanity would be blessed (Gn 22:18). At first this saving help of God is shown in concrete material ways, most notably in the liberation of the Chosen People from slavery in Egypt. However, over time the prophets would raise the eyes of Israel toward a more profound saving help to be granted in the future, particularly through the coming of the future Messiah.

The Hebrew People initially saw God's saving action in a collective perspective, that is, toward the people as a whole. With time, they came to understand this action in a more spiritual and individual dimension. Through the prophet Jeremiah, God announces the future covenant he will make with his people, which is "not like the covenant which I made with their fathers when I took them by the hand to bring them out of the land of Egypt" (Jer 31:32). This covenant, rather, will be more interior: "I will put my law within them, and I will write it upon their hearts; and I will be their God, and they shall be my people" (v. 33). Each individual member of the people would come to share in this intimacy: "No longer shall each man teach his neighbor and each his brother, saying, 'Know the Lord,' for they shall all know me, from the least of them to the greatest, says the Lord" (v. 34).

The Old Testament summarizes the effect of God's grace upon man, in both the material and spiritual sense, with the word *blessing*. Through his blessing, God wants to grant life, peace, and fecundity to man (see, for example, Nm 6:24–26). God takes the initiative in establishing a friendship with his people and freeing them from sin. At the same time, God's grace asks for a concrete response. God wants his people to respond to the law, given to them in the covenant, and so to share in God's justice or holiness.

While many key aspects of the New Testament notion of grace are found in the Old Testament, the Hebrew Scriptures do not make a specific distinction between grace, understood as God's loving attitude toward man, and grace understood as a specific gift that God grants to man. Nor does the Old Testament distinguish clearly between the natural and supernatural orders, or between the spiritual and material gifts. Each of these realities is seen as part of God's gratuitous and loving action. The true nature of grace, as a specific gift by which God allows us to participate in his own divine life, was yet to be fully revealed.

Grace in the New Testament

the concept of grace has deep roots in the Old hich God enters into friendship with a peo- s saving help. Still, the word *grace*—the Greek s a radically new action by which God has life of man through Jesus Christ and through Holy Spirit. In Christ, God has definitively r, steadfast love, graciousness, and faithfulness. e writers of the New Testament have an acute s reality, many of them do not specifically use the word *charis*. The word does not appear in the Gospels of St. Matthew and St. Mark; in John's Gospel it appears only in the Prologue. The accounts of Matthew and Mark, nonetheless, show the foundation for the Christian term *grace* in their revelation that the kingdom of God has drawn close to men through the Person of Jesus Christ.

This kingdom is not an earthly institution. Rather, it comes about by a radical new invitation to turn to God in faith and to be freed from sin (Mk 1:15). In Christ, God has revealed his fatherly love for us in a new way and invites us to share in his own divine life in an unprecedented manner. Christ reveals that God is a father, ever attentive to the needs of mankind, and moreover Christ grants us the possibility of participating in his own unique filiation with the eternal Father (Mt 6:32; 11:27). In the face of the Pharisees' conception of holiness, which heavily emphasized man's efforts to carry out the law, Christ manifests God's wholly gratuitous love for sinners.

Paul uses the word *grace* (*charis*) as a central concept for expressing the new revelation of God which has taken place through the Incarnation and saving passion of the Son of God. With this term, the Apostle of the Gentiles seeks to express the reality of God's gracious love in a way which would be understandable to a non-Jewish audience. In the Greek world of Christ's time, the word *charis* had come to indicate a ruler's gracious favor, as well as a specific gift that was the result of this benevolent attitude. The word had even come to be associated with a kind of religious power that came from the world above.

All of these resonances made *charis* a fitting term to articulate the immense favor of God toward man which has taken place in the Person of Christ, and also for expressing the way man himself is transformed and elevated by this action of God. Paul uses the word in various senses. In the first place, it can refer broadly to the entire mystery of salvation accomplished in Christ. Christ is "the grace" that God the Father has bestowed on man. The apostle describes the entire mystery of Christ when he states that "the grace of God has appeared for the salvation of all men" (Ti 2:11). With the term *grace*, the apostle emphasizes the immense goodness that God has shown to us without any preceding merit on our part.

Paul expresses this gratuitousness of God in a striking way in his Letter to the Ephesians: "But God, who is rich in mercy, out of the great love with which he loved us, even when we were dead through our trespasses, made us alive together with Christ (by grace [*chariti*] you have been saved)" (2:4–5). The apostle wants to accentuate this loving divine initiative to those Jews who seek salvation in the fulfillment of the law, and also to those pagans who seek salvation in a special religious knowledge outside of Christ.

Today as well, we can run the risk of reducing religion to a set of practices, whose completion gives a set of satisfaction in our own efforts. In the face of such a tendency, in the same passage Paul goes on to describe how God has shown "the immeasurable riches of his grace in kindness toward us in Christ Jesus." The apostle then notes, even more resolutely, the absolute primacy of God's action over that of man: "For by grace you have been saved through faith; and this is not your own doing, it is the gift of God—not because of works, lest any man should boast" (Eph 2:7–9). Grace here serves as a pivotal way of expressing the radical gift offered to us through the Christian religion, which we are called to receive in faith. More than anything that the Christian might *do*, he is first called to let himself receive what God himself has *done* in his loving plan of salvation.

In addition to this more general sense of grace, as a way of describing and characterizing the entire mystery of Christ, Paul also describes grace with a more particular meaning. In this usage, grace can refer to each specific help offered by God to the believer. Later in the same Letter to the Ephesians, the apostle speaks of the different tasks through which the Church is built up. He comments that "grace was given to each of us according to the measure of Christ's gift" (4:7).

While we have seen that the concept of grace shows us the radical initiative of God's love, grace is always more than simply an action of God. Grace implies God's will to reach the human person; it is precisely the way we try to convey God's mysterious desire to give us a *sharing* in his own life. Grace introduces a totally new principle of life into man, which destroys the power of sin: "Where sin increased, grace abounded all the more, so that, as sin reigned in death, grace also might reign through righteousness to eternal life through Jesus Christ our Lord" (Rom 5:20–21).

Since grace in a wider sense refers to the gift of God which is Christ himself, to live in grace means fundamentally to live *in Christ Jesus*. Paul writes to the Galatians that "it is no longer I who live, but Christ who lives in me" (2:20). Grace therefore means a life of divine sonship through the only begotten Son of God, and furthermore a sharing in the Holy Spirit, the divine Person who is the love between the Father and the Son.

The powerful action of God in man, through grace, is meant to bear fruit in *works*. While Paul emphasizes the absolute priority of God's action, he also reminds the Ephesians that they are called to respond to God's "work" in them with their own "works," the result of freely cooperating with God's action: "For we are his workmanship, created in Christ Jesus for good works, which God prepared beforehand, that we should walk in them" (Eph 2:10). Grace leads the Christian to a specific way of life guided by the Holy Spirit, characterized by "faith working through love" (Gal 5:6).

The word *grace* does not appear frequently in the writings of John. Nonetheless, this Evangelist, using different language, refers to the same fundamental reality. Rather than *grace*, this apostle chooses to use the word *life* to express the same saving action of God toward men. As in the case of the word *grace*, *life* applies particularly to the Second Person of the Trinity, the Word: "In him was life, and the life was the light of men" (Jn 1:4).

Christ is "life" not simply because he is alive, but because as God he is the source of all life. John uses the Greek word *zoe* for *life*, which suggests a vital, spiritual principle that animates human life. By contrast, the other Greek word for *life*, *bios*, refers to a specific human life or the duration of life. Hence, John's use of the word expresses the way the believer comes to a new sharing in the life of God himself by means of faith.

John's Gospel strongly emphasizes how we are raised to life through the coming of Christ: "For God so loved the world that he gave his only Son, that whoever believes in him should not perish but have eternal life" (3:16). This "eternal life" is nothing less than a very participation in the life of God, through faith: "This is eternal life, that they know thee the only true God, and Jesus Christ whom thou hast sent" (Jn 17:3).

With the language of "grace" and "life," Paul and John seek to express the radical new reality which has come into the world through Jesus Christ. Through the coming of the Word made flesh, God has demonstrated his love for us and given us a new principle of being and acting. Later generations of Christians would continue to reflect on this powerful and mysterious action of God in the life of believers.

Dimensions of the Life of Grace

Over the course of the centuries after Christ, as we shall explore in more detail in later chapters, theologians developed a set of concepts that help us to appreciate aspects of what grace is. Since *grace* is a word by which we try to describe the mysterious action of God in the believer, none of these concepts can fully express the reality of what grace is. Still, they permit us to better understand the mystery of how God acts in the believer and elevates him to the supernatural life.

Thomas Aquinas understood grace as *created grace*. This expression does not mean that grace is something created. Rather, this concept helps to communicate how we are given a new being through grace. The idea of created grace allows us to distinguish this action of God within man from *uncreated grace*, which refers to God himself, the source of all grace.

Created grace expresses the way our powers are raised up to live a supernatural existence of faith, hope, and love. At the same time, this supernatural life leads us to a new closeness to the uncreated gift by which we are reborn as sons and daughters of God. This uncreated gift is the Holy Spirit, who dwells in the soul of the Christian.

We can articulate other particular aspects of how grace works in the life of the Christian. We can examine grace from the perspective of how this divine help brings about a true identification with Christ. This new presence of Christ purifies the soul of sin, and from this point of view we can identify another important aspect of the action of grace, which is *justification*. Justification refers to the specific action through which God forgives the offense of sin and re-establishes friendship with us. Justification implies the forgiveness of sin, but the faith of the Church sees this action as more than simply the elimination of the guilt due to sin. Justification involves an authentic interior transformation of the person.

We can refer to this new state of the person, after justification, with the term *sanctifying grace* or *habitual grace*. These terms indicate something more than simply a help that is granted by God to a person at a given moment. They imply that the human being is elevated, in a stable or habitual way, to a new state of participation in the divine life. This habitual state is distinct from *actual graces*, which are the specific gifts God grants to us at specific moments so as to carry out particular actions.

Theologians have also distinguished between *healing grace* (known as *gratia sanans* in Latin) and *elevating grace* (*gratia elevans*). These terms refer to two aspects of the single reality of grace. Healing grace refers to grace insofar as it heals our human nature from the wounds of sin, while elevating grace indicates the special help by which God raises us to communion with the divine life.

The New Testament manifests the way divine life comes to us particularly through the sacraments. We can use the term *sacramental grace* to describe that grace that comes to us in this way. Sacraments "are efficacious signs of grace, instituted by Christ and entrusted to the Church, by which divine life is dispensed to us." They are a privileged means by which Christ offers the gift of grace so as to sanctify human life and thus make the Christian's entire life a "spiritual worship," which is "holy and acceptable to God" (Rom 12:1).

Through the sacrament of baptism, the believer receives a new birth through water and the Spirit, so as become a child of God (Jn 1:12, 3:5); the sacrament of confirmation increases and deepens this baptismal grace, through a special outpouring of the Holy Spirit. The sacrament of the Eucharist nourishes the Christian's supernatural life, and at the same time points to the fullness of life at the final resurrection: "He who eats my flesh and drinks my blood has eternal life, and I will raise him up at the last day" (Jn 6:54). The special grace of the sacrament of reconciliation brings about forgiveness and healing for sins, while the grace of the sacrament of anointing bestows help for the believer to face illness and old age.

The other two sacraments, in different ways, provide grace in order to live out specific missions that are particularly vital for the service of the Church. The sacrament of ordination brings with it a unique grace to configure its recipient to Christ, so as to serve him in the ministry of deacon, priest, or bishop. The sacrament of matrimony imparts a special grace that aids married couples, so that they may sanctify their human love and that this love might truly be a reflection of Christ's love for his Church.

In the coming chapters we shall have the opportunity to study various aspects of grace in more detail. We shall do so, looking above all to Christ, the source of all grace. Jesus Christ is truly God, and as God he does not need to receive grace. However, as Christ is fully man, his human nature does have grace. This grace comes from the unity of the divine nature and the human nature in the one Person of Christ.

In the Prologue of his Gospel, John tells us that "the Word became flesh and dwelt among us, full of grace and truth" (1:14). When the Word, the Second Person of the Trinity, took on a human nature, this same human nature was filled with grace, so that this human nature might be the source of grace for the entire human race. God the Son wanted to accept the reality of grace in his human nature, not for his own sake, but so that our human nature might participate in the life of God.

The profound truth of the reality of grace, in which God has wanted us to share in the reality of his life, is shown to us in the Blessed Virgin Mary. By God's design, she has served as a unique mediator in the process by which grace filled the human nature of Christ. In the moment of the Annunciation, the archangel Gabriel greets her with the Greek word *kecharitomene*, which has traditionally been translated as "full of grace." As the twentieth-century Belgian biblical scholar Ignace de la Potterie pointed out, this phrase describes grace not simply in its origin in God but also in its effect on the Blessed Virgin. "Full of grace" refers not simply to the graces that Mary will receive at the moment of the Incarnation, but also to the grace that she has *already* received in light of her future mission as Mother of God.

Mary, a fully human creature, manifests the fullest realization of the reality that God wants to elevate the person to share in the divine life. God wanted Mary, in her perfect holiness, to share in the mediating function that is carried out fully and uniquely by her Son. Therefore, our reflections on the mystery of grace must ever keep in mind the role that she has, along with her Son, in leading us to a participation in the divine life. As Vatican II's Constitution on the Church affirmed, "She is our mother in the order of grace."

CHAPTER 3

Grace as Indwelling of the Holy Spirit

The Holy Spirit as Uncreated Gift

At the back of St. Peter's Basilica in Rome stands the *Chair of St. Peter*, a magnificent seventeenth-century sculpture monument by the Italian artist Gian Lorenzo Bernini. The artwork provides an elaborate casing to the wooden chair, which has been venerated as the chair from which Peter taught. The monument is a splendid testimony to the Catholic notion of grace. Rays of divine light and golden clouds, surrounded by angels, express the mysterious action of God that gives his strength to the Vicar of Christ and the Church. Those rays of light, and not the four doctors of the church that stand to the right and left of the chair, are the force that upholds St. Peter's chair.

At the rear of the artwork, Bernini depicted the source of all this divine action: the Holy Spirit. An oval window portrays the Third Person of the Trinity in the traditional symbolism of a dove. The image reminds us that the Holy Spirit is the animating principle behind the abundant action of grace in the life of the Church. In this chapter, we will examine the intimate relationship between grace and this divine Person.

Medieval theologians described the Holy Spirit as "uncreated gift." The term *uncreated*, as we saw in the last chapter, served to distinguish God himself from that action of God in man which we describe with the term *grace*, which we can consider as a *created gift*. The distinction between these two forms of gift drew from the theological reflection on Paul's statement, in the Letter to the Romans, that "God's love has been poured into our hearts through the Holy Spirit who has been given to us" (5:5). The twelfth-century theologian Peter Lombard, who taught in Paris and whose books of *Sentences* had great authority in the medieval period, interpreted this text to mean that the Holy Spirit is *both* the love of the Father and the Son *and* the love through which we love God and others. This opinion brought about a lively debate among theologians in subsequent years.

Lombard's position helps us to see the connection between the love present in God himself and the charity Christians are called to live. Still, his interpretation is problematic. If the Holy Spirit is simply the love with which we love, then love would not be a virtue that forms part of our being. The Holy Spirit is, after all, fully God and therefore radically distinct from us, who are creatures.

With time, the debate regarding Lombard's position led theologians to appreciate that charity is a virtue that is not the same as the Holy Spirit. Charity is a *stable* disposition or habit that forms part of the person, rather than being God himself.

While the acts of knowing and loving God is an act of the person, these acts are made possible—as Thomas Aquinas points out—by the action of God himself. Among the Persons of the Trinity, we can attribute to the Holy Spirit the particular act by which God gives of himself so that we might share in the divine life. This is because, within the life of the Trinity itself, the Holy Spirit proceeds from the Father and the Son.

The New Testament never tells us that the Holy Spirit is begotten by the Father, as in the case of the Son, who is the "only Son" of the Father (Jn 3:16). Rather the Holy Spirit proceeds from the Father (Jn 15:26). In light of Christ's promise that he will "send" the Holy Spirit to believers (Jn 15:26), the Church has recognized that the Holy Spirit also proceeds from the Son. The Greek word for proceed literally means "to cause to go out" or "to depart." Based on the suggestions present in Sacred Scripture, the Christian tradition has identified this specific movement of the Holy Spirit with a procession of *love*. As Aquinas points out, love is a force which moves or impels a person to carry out a given action, and so it is a fitting term to describe the procession of the Third Divine Person. Additionally, as a gift is a sign of gratuitous love, the term *gift* has also come to be a specific name for the Holy Spirit.

These considerations can help us to appreciate the intimate relationship between the Holy Spirit and the mysterious reality of God's action in man known as grace, even if grace and the Holy Spirit are different realities. Grace refers more specifically to the human condition or state, elevated by God's action, while the Holy Spirit is fully God and transcendent to us. Grace is some*thing*, while the Holy Spirit is some*one*. In the remainder of this chapter, we will examine the way in which grace brings about a new relationship between us and the Third Divine Person.

The Holy Spirit as Gift of God to Man in the Old Testament

The opening verses of Scripture testify to the "the Spirit of God" which "was moving over the face of the waters" (Gn 1:2). The Hebrew word for "spirit," *ruah*, could refer to a breath from the mouth or to the wind, as well as to the principle that gives life to man. John Paul II points out that even this initial reference to *spirit*, before the Creation of man, suggests the beginning of God's desire to share his very life with us.

God's creation of man with a "breath" of his own life (Gn 2:7) prefigures this intimacy.

Later, the term *spirit* would also refer to a new gift which God promised to man. In the face of the unfaithfulness of his people, God promises "a new heart" and "a new spirit" (Ez 36:26). This spirit is not simply biological life, but a new moral strength through which God will "cause" the People of God to walk in his statutes and to be careful to observe his ordinances (Ez 36:27). This outpouring of the Spirit will lead to a new closeness between God and Israel: "You shall dwell in the land which I gave to your fathers; and you shall be my people, and I will be your God" (Ez 36:28).

The Old Testament manifests the divine spirit as a special interior force which God grants to special figures in the history of salvation, such as Moses (Nm 11:17) and David (1 Sm 16:13). At the same time, this gift of the spirit upon certain persons is meant to reach all of humanity. Some of that spirit which God sends upon Moses later descends upon the seventy elders of Israel, and later yet upon two others who were not present in that larger group. Moses exclaims: "Would that all the LORD's people were prophets, that the LORD would put his spirit upon them!" (Nm 11:29).

This desire of the great patriarch would become a reality in the times to come. The prophet Isaiah foretells that the Spirit of the Lord would dwell in a special way upon the Messiah (Is 11:1–2) and be the source of a new righteousness, which would spread its fruits to all peoples (Is 11:6–12). In the prophet Joel's description of the "day of the Lord," the moment of God's definitive saving action, the Holy Spirit will descend upon "all flesh" (Jl 2:28).

God's promise of the Holy Spirit is closely connected to his desire to make his *presence* among his people. The Chosen

People recognized themselves to be the special place where God had "settled" (Ex 24:16). This presence was made tangible through the pillar of cloud that went before the people of Israel as they traveled through the desert, in the tabernacle that the people carried, and later in the temple.

All of these places, however sacred they are, prepare the way for a more definitive dwelling of God with his people (2 Sm 7:13, 16). This special closeness would require a new outpouring of the spirit by God, which would come about in the times of the Messiah.

The Promise and Gift of the Spirit in the New Testament

The Gospels clearly reveal Christ to be the Messiah, upon whom God's Spirit dwells (Lk 4:18). With the Incarnation, God's presence among his people comes to a new level in the human nature of Christ. As John declares, "the Word became flesh and dwelt among us" (Jn 1:14). The word *dwelt* in Greek literally means to "encamp" or "to live in a tent" and recalls the Old Testament tent of meeting, where God made his presence among the people of Israel.

St. Luke also makes use of Old Testament imagery to express the new presence of God which has been brought about through the Incarnation. In the moment of the Annunciation, Mary appears as the New Tabernacle in which God dwells among his people in a way that far surpasses the first tabernacle, which contained the ark of the covenant. This ark, which originally held the two stone tablets upon which the Ten Commandments had been engraved, was the special sign of God's special bond with his people. At the moment of the Annunciation, the Holy Spirit overshadows Mary (Lk 1:35) just as the cloud of God's presence had covered the Old Testament Tabernacle (Ex 40:35).

Such imagery helps us to understand how God's presence among mankind has been realized in a radically new way through the mystery of the Incarnation. These scriptural expressions also help us to reflect on the dwelling of God in the soul of the Christian which comes about as a result of the action of grace. This presence is a presence of all three divine Persons: the Father, the Son, and the Holy Spirit. At the same time, Scripture and the Christian tradition specifically associate this presence with the Holy Spirit, who, as we have considered, is the fruit of an eternal procession of divine love from the Father and the Son.

While earlier episodes in the life of Christ, such as the Annunciation, offer hints of the special role of the Holy Spirit in the souls of Christ's disciples, it is only at the Last Supper that the true nature of the Paraclete—the Greek term for the Third Divine Person—and his presence in the Christian are more fully manifested.

As John Paul II observes, the timing of this revelation has a special significance. The Last Supper is the moment in which Christ anticipates the paschal mystery, the mystery which includes the passion, death, and resurrection of Christ, as well as Christ's exaltation and sending of the Holy Spirit. Christ communicates this mystery in a sacramental way, before these events actually take place, through the institution of the Holy Eucharist. Christ also chose this same moment to speak of his gift of the Holy Spirit to the Church, and thus reveal the intimate closeness which the Trinity desires to have with man.

In response to the petition of the apostle Philip—"Lord, show us the Father, and we shall be satisfied" (Jn 14:8)—Jesus responds with the affirmation that the Father dwells in the

Son, and further that this same inhabitation of the Father, along with the Son, will become a reality in the life of Christ's followers: "I will pray the Father, and he will give you another Counselor, to be with you for ever, even the Spirit of truth, whom the world cannot receive, because it neither sees him nor knows him; you know him, for he dwells with you, and will be in you" (Jn 14:16–17). Here, Jesus names the Holy Spirit with the Greek word *Parakleton*, a word which does not appear in the Greek version of the Old Testament, nor in the New Testament except for the writings of John. The term was used in the ancient Greek world, before Christ, to refer to a helper or assistant, especially in the legal context. Elsewhere, John describes Christ himself with the same Greek word to remind us that Christ himself is our "advocate" for mercy before the Father (1 Jn 2:1).

In the case of the text from the Last Supper, Christ speaks of "another Counselor." While Christ himself remains the advocate for us before the Father, Christ promises to send "another advocate" who will be present in the soul of the disciples in a new way: "You know him, for he dwells with you, and will be in you" (Jn 14:17). The New Testament specifically identifies the Holy Spirit as the protagonist behind the action of grace, through which God enters into the human heart, redeems it, and raises it to communion with the divine life. In this way, the Holy Spirit brings to completion Christ's redemption. As John Paul II comments, while this redemption is totally carried out by Christ, "this Redemption is, at the same time, constantly carried out in human hearts and minds—in the history of the world—by the Holy Spirit, who is the 'other Counselor.'"

While Scripture identifies the Holy Spirit as the divine Person responsible for the interior action of God in the heart of man—"No one can say 'Jesus is Lord' except by the Holy Spirit" (1 Cor 12:3)—the words of Christ also indicate that the Father and the Son will also come to make their dwelling within the Christian. In response to the question of the apostle Jude, Christ responds: "If a man loves me, he will keep my word, and my Father will love him, and we will come to him and make our home with him" (Jn 14:23). In these words, Christ reveals a special presence which he and the Father will continue to have in the soul of the disciple, even after Jesus has departed. The action of the Paraclete brings about the miracle by which Christ can depart and "go the Father" (Jn 14:12), and yet at the same time remain with his disciples. As Christ goes on to say, the Holy Spirit is the one who will lead the disciples to a remembrance of Christ (Jn 14:26); the Holy Spirit will take that which is Christ's and declare it to the disciples (Jn 16:15).

In light of this testimony of Christ, we can ask: If the Father and the Son continue to be present in the soul of the Christian, why does Scripture attribute God's action in the soul specifically to the Holy Spirit? St. Augustine, the great North African bishop and doctor of the church who lived in the city of Hippo, points out that the Holy Spirit is the love with which the Father loves the Son and with which the Son loves the Father. This affirmation is based on the testimony of Scripture. John tells us that "God is love" (1 Jn 4:8), and, in light of John's letter, Augustine asserts that we abide in God by abiding in love. Moreover, the bishop of Hippo goes on to state, John connects this love with the Holy Spirit when he says: "By this we know that we abide in him and he in us, because he has given us of his own Spirit" (1 Jn 4:13). Augustine also cites for his argument the words of Paul, which, as we have seen, became an important reference point during the

Scholastic period: "God's love has been poured into our hearts through the Holy Spirit who has been given to us" (Rom 5:5).

In light of this scriptural and patristic perspective, we can better grasp how the third divine Person bears a special relationship with the action of grace. Grace is ultimately the overflow of God's own love, which has brought humankind into existence and seeks to raise us to a sharing in the divine life. This overflow bears a certain resemblance with the Holy Spirit's own identity within the Trinity. In the inner life of the Trinity, the Holy Spirit is the divine Person through whom the Father and Son love one another.

The existence of the Third Divine Person, as manifested in Scripture, shows how the love of the Father and the Son involves a procession—within the life of the Trinity—of another divine Person who is gift. John Paul II affirms that "in the Holy Spirit the intimate life of the Triune God becomes totally gift, an exchange of mutual love between the divine Persons," and moreover that "through the Holy Spirit God exists in the mode of gift." It is fitting, then, that the Holy Spirit is that gift through which we come to share in the Trinitarian life.

The Holy Spirit's special action in the life of the Christian shows us how God's plan of salvation is a free act of that love through which the Father, the Son, and the Holy Spirit exist in a perfect communion of divine love. As John Paul II also notes, the Holy Spirit, while being one with the Father and the Son in one divine substance, "is love and uncreated gift from which derives as from its source . . . all giving of gifts vis-a-vis creatures." These gifts include both the very act of coming into being through Creation as well as the gift of grace. The Holy Spirit is that fundamental model and source, then, which we must always see in close relationship with the mysterious action of grace in the soul.

The Holy Spirit's Presence and the Indwelling of the Trinity in the Soul

The words of Christ at the Last Supper, as we have seen, disclose the desire of Christ, along with the Father, to "make our home" (Jn 14:23) in the Christian; we have also seen how the Holy Spirit has a special role in this presence of God within the soul. Paul has a deep awareness of this same reality, recognizing that the Spirit which dwells within the Christian is the principle of a new life of holiness as a son of God (Rom 8:9–16). He exhorts the Corinthians to act in accord with this presence: "Do you not know that your body is a temple of the Holy Spirit within you, which you have from God?" (1 Cor 6:19).

This presence of the Holy Spirit is the source of a new life which Paul describes as a life "in Christ." He reminds the Galatians that "as many of you as were baptized into Christ have put on Christ" (3:27). Along with this presence of the Holy Spirit and the Son is that of God the Father, as "God has sent the Spirit of his Son into our hearts, crying, 'Abba! Father!'" (Gal 4:6).

From these scriptural references, we can comprehend how the New Testament clearly affirms the presence of the three divine Persons in the soul, while at the same time attributing this presence to the particular action of the Paraclete. Over the centuries, Christians have reflected on this mysterious indwelling of the Trinity in the soul. While God's revelation leads us to know this reality, this truth has not been easy to describe.

Thomas Aquinas explains that while God is present in all things as their Creator, through grace he becomes present in the person in a special way, as the object known is in the knower and the beloved is in the lover. Grace allows the person to come to know and love God, and these actions are only possible through the presence of the Holy Spirit in the person.

Through this presence, as Aquinas states, God dwells in the person as in his own temple. Furthermore, as the Dominican saint points out elsewhere, the divine Persons have their own special way of presence with the person. The gift of wisdom brings the person to identification with Christ, whom we can appropriately call the wisdom of God. The gift of love allows the person to act according to the Holy Spirit, the divine Person who is the love of the Father and the Son.

In this perspective, we can say that the presence of the Holy Trinity in the soul is the source of the person's ability to live a supernatural life of faith, hope, and love. This life is directed toward the Holy Trinity. In addition to being the source and end of the life of grace, the Holy Trinity further shapes the person's way of acting according to God's own being. In an ineffable manner, without taking away a person's own identity, the Holy Trinity shapes a person's way of knowing and acting according to God's own wisdom and love. The believer's new way of life, through which he can attain to the knowledge of God's inner life and participate in a communion of love with the Trinity, implies a presence of the three divine Persons in the depths of the person's soul.

Many theologians have understood this new state of the creature, in which the Trinity dwells, in relation to the special grace of God enjoyed by the blessed in heaven. Aquinas teaches that a "light of glory" (*lumen gloriae*) is needed for the person to come to experience the immediate contemplation of God in heavenly glory. Through this special illumination, God gives the person a new capacity to come to this vision of God.

This direct perception of God in heaven will not be a completely new experience for the Christian. Through the gift of grace, we experience a beginning of close personal union with the Holy Trinity. As Pope Leo XIII observed, the Holy Trinity's presence within the soul brings about a union of charity with God which differs "only in degree or state from that with which God beatifies the saints in heaven." This indwelling of God in the soul, which is attributed particularly to the Holy Spirit, brings about an intimate and affectionate closeness of faith, hope, and love to the divine Persons. This supernatural life of the Christian on earth is a beginning of that full communion with God which the saints in heaven experience.

Over the centuries, theologians have offered many explanations of how exactly the Trinity can make its presence within us. As Pope Pius XII notes, this mystery goes beyond the power of our understanding and expression. He cautioned Christians against an exaggerated vision of God's presence in the soul, which would eliminate the distinction between God and his creatures. Nonetheless, this mid-twentieth-century pope invited Christians to contemplate the profound truth that the divine Persons dwell within us. In a way that goes beyond all understanding, and "in a unique and very intimate manner which transcends all created nature," he affirms that the divine Persons are present in human beings and that Christians can enter into a relationship of knowledge and love with these same divine Persons.

By the Trinity's presence in the soul of the Christian, God has fulfilled the Old Testament promise to make his presence in his people, and he has done so in a way which exceeds anything that man could imagine. The soul of each Christian, and no longer the Old Testament tabernacle or Jewish temple, is the special place in which God dwells. Through this inhabitation, God raises the person to a new level of being; through the gift of the Holy Spirit, as John Paul II commented, "human life becomes permeated, through participation, by the divine life, and itself acquires a divine, supernatural dimension."

Therefore, as we examine the reality of grace through which our own being is elevated to the divine life, we should seek to understand this reality in close connection with a special presence of the Trinity in the core of our own being. This presence, the fruit of the Holy Spirit's special action, is the source of the Christian's supernatural way of being and acting.

While the indwelling of the Holy Spirit is a stable presence in the soul, this presence is at the same time a constant source of dynamism. The Second Vatican Council's Constitution on the Church, *Lumen Gentium*, noted that "the Spirit dwells in the Church and in the hearts of the faithful, as in a temple." The Council went on to say that this presence leads to an abundant and manifold action through which the Church spreads the work of Christ's redemption. In the faithful, as the constitution notes, the Holy Spirit "prays on their behalf and bears witness to the fact that they are adopted sons."

The action of the Holy Spirit works in the structure that Christ established for the Church, which includes the sacraments and ministries, but also *charisms*. The word for "charism" in Greek is *charisma*, which means "free gift" and is related to the same root word as grace, *charis*. Charisms are special gifts that are the fruit of the Holy Spirit's presence in the Church, and by them the Paraclete builds up the Church in a variety of ways. As Paul writes to the Corinthians, "there are varieties of gifts, but the same Spirit," and "to each is given the manifestation of the Spirit for the common good" (1 Cor 12:4, 7).

Many Christians today are interested in charisms and in a "charismatic" way of life, inspired by the Holy Spirit. This lively interest, to the extent that it is authentic (there are false charisms that are really works of men rather than the Holy Spirit), is a sign of the Spirit's continual presence.

At the same time, these special gifts need to be viewed in communion with the Church's structure, which is also a sign of the Spirit's presence. The Magisterium has the sole authority to determine the authenticity of new charisms and spiritualities that emerge among the People of God. Through these various charisms or gifts, as *Lumen Gentium* states, the Holy Spirit "makes the Church keep the freshness of youth." In these ways, the indwelling of the Holy Trinity constantly exercises its influence in the heart of man, while always respecting his freedom.

The Presence of the Holy Spirit and the "Divinization" of Man

The Greek-speaking Fathers of the Church, reflecting on the truth of God's presence in the soul of the Christian, developed the notion that man is "divinized" through the Holy Spirit's redeeming action in the soul. We might find this notion problematic if we were to examine it from a philosophical point of view. The Christian is not "divinized" in the strict sense, since he does not become God. As an important New Testament text on this theme states, Christians are made "partakers of the divine nature" (2 Pt 1:4); they enter into communion with this nature but they themselves do not take on the status of being God.

Still, many Fathers of the Church found that the language of "divinization" was a powerful way of expressing the fact that the Christian is truly elevated to a sharing in the divine life, through God the Son's sharing in a genuine human nature. We can truly say that the Christian is divinized, if by this we mean that through grace we share in the promise of the future resurrection, we are capable of contemplating God, we unite ourselves to God through the sacraments, and we can act in a divine way through works of charity.

St. Athanasius, the fourth-century bishop of Alexandria, succinctly stated that Christ "assumed humanity that we might become God." This perspective was inspired in part by the philosophy of Plato, which appreciated the human soul's likeness to God. But above all, the notion of man's divinization grew out of a profound meditation on man's identification with God, as described in the Scriptures and brought about through the sacraments. Augustine remarks, in his commentary on the Gospel of John: "Let us rejoice, then, and give thanks that we are not only Christians, but Christ."

Among those Christian traditions which developed in the Eastern part of Christianity, the notion of divinization has become an important way of expressing how man is raised to the divine life. Christians in these traditions, which include the Orthodox, prefer to use the idea of divinization, instead of grace, to describe how the believer is transformed through the action of the Holy Spirit.

This Eastern perspective has the advantage of reminding us of the mystery of God's presence in the believer, and of the need for a sense of adoration and contemplation before this presence. The Western point of view, by contrast, is more focused on grace and how we ourselves participate in the life of God. From this Western point of view, the idea of divinization can make it seem difficult to distinguish between God and the creature. In any case, no human language can totally express the richness and mystery of our union with God.

John Paul II encouraged the Church to learn from the sense of mystery characteristic of Eastern Christians, who "perceive that one draws close to this presence [that of the Holy Trinity] above all by letting oneself be taught an adoring silence, for at the culmination of the knowledge and experience of God is his absolute transcendence." This spiritual tradition reminds us that while the theological notion of sanctifying grace can be a valuable way of understanding God's action in the soul, only a contemplative attitude of prayer can allow us to grasp more deeply the mystery of the Holy Trinity's action in the soul of the believer. There the Holy Spirit dwells and acts in the innermost being of the Christian, in a way which surpasses all understanding.

CHAPTER 4

Grace as Divine Filiation in Christ

IN THE LAST CHAPTER, we examined the gift of grace in particular relation to the Third Person of the Trinity, the Holy Spirit. The Holy Spirit shows us the overflow of love which is contained in God's own inner life, and which comes forth from that divine life so as to draw human beings into a new and intimate communion with the Trinity.

This special action of the Third Divine Person leads the believer into a new relationship with God the Father and God the Son, which we express with the concept of *divine filiation*. Through the mysterious action of the Paraclete, the Christian shares in the eternal relationship of filiation that exists from the Son to the Father, and as a result we call the Christian an adopted son of God. In this chapter we will explore this reality in more detail.

God as Father in the Old Testament

By his plan of salvation, God desires to lead men and women to their ultimate destiny as children of God. At the same time, the revelation of this truth was gradual and required a profound purification of what exactly "fatherhood" and "sonship" mean with regard to God.

The invocation of God as father has been a common practice in religion since ancient times. Ancient Indian religion, as well as Greek and Roman religion, turned to God as "father"; this notion was connected with the awareness that God had brought life into being. In ancient Hindu culture, *Dyaus*, the Sanskrit word for the sky and also the "father of light" or the sun, is considered to be a "father" who paired with mother earth (*Prthivi*) to give rise to vegetation and all life. *Dyaus* is at the root of various words for God, including *Zeus* in Greek and *Deus* in Latin. The Greek god Zeus was also known as father and as universal god. This god, like *Dyaus*, had human characteristics. Greek mythology portrayed Zeus as having many human passions, including anger.

From these ways of recognizing God's fatherly presence, we can appreciate how the notion of God as a father could easily lend itself to misunderstandings. Certainly, it is natural to think of God in terms of a father, the male parent who cooperates in bringing new human life into the world. Still, this association could lead to a concept of God as little more than a human father.

In this context, we can appreciate why the Old Testament does not often use the word *father* to describe God. Much more often, the term refers to the human fathers who had such a key role in ancient Jewish society. While fatherhood is a concept familiar to us, in the Old Testament God reveals himself to be the God who is above all human conceptions. God describes himself to Moses as "I Am Who I Am" (Ex 3:14). Through this title, God reveals his nature to his people but also shows that he is infinitely above all of our efforts to comprehend him. He is "holy," which means that he is transcendent and separate from any reality that is not God (Lv 11:44).

However, while fatherhood does not form part of the core idea of God among the Jewish people, a number of texts from the Old Testament make indirect reference to God's fatherhood. These texts do not specifically identify God's essence as being a father; rather, they compare God's action to that of a human father. God reveals to Moses that Israel is his "first-born son" (Ex 4:22). The psalmist affirms that "as a father pities his children, so the LORD pities those who fear him" (Ps 103:13). Such references to God as father are a way of making use of a very familiar figure in society, as a way of describing the love and concern of God for his people.

Such texts manifest an awareness that God acts in a fatherly way, but in a way profoundly different from the notions of God's fatherhood which were present among the pagan religions. God does not show his fatherhood through acting like a human father but through his transcendent and divine power. During the exodus of Israel, God shows himself to be a father who acted as lord, protector, and provider to the Chosen People. In light of this truth, the Chosen People affirm to God that "thou, O LORD, art our Father, our Redeemer from of old is thy name" (Is 63:16). This loving care of God for the people as a whole led them to appreciate that each just person could also be considered a son of God (see, for example, Sir 23:1–4).

The loving, fatherly care of God for the people of Israel as a whole was also particularly expressed in the special fatherly relationship of God to the king. The notion of the king as God's son was common in the ancient world, but the people of Israel understood this sonship in a more spiritual way. God's fatherly care for the king would give rise to a kingdom of moral rectitude, a kingdom of which there would be no end (2 Sm 7:13–14).

Overall, the concept of fatherhood was not the dominant way in which the Old Testament People of God understood the nature of God. As the twentieth-century German scripture scholar Gottfried Quell pointed out, the Old Testament makes "only comparatively sparing use" of this notion in relation to God. The concept of fatherhood in relation to God needed to be purified from many possible misunderstandings. Still, the Chosen People could not help but use this image to express the love and tenderness that God had shown to his people. This awareness of fatherhood would lay the groundwork for a radically new manifestation of fatherhood in Jesus Christ.

God as Father in the New Testament

The manifestation of God's eternal fatherhood, by means of his only begotten Son, is a central message of the Gospel. While the language of fatherhood is present in both the Old and New Testaments, the perspective is nonetheless radically distinct.

In the Old Testament, the key reference point for fatherhood is the human figure of the father, which was so vital to ancient Jewish culture. In the New Testament, Christ reveals God as the Father in the fullest sense and the model for human fatherhood. Paul kneels "before the Father, from whom every family in heaven and on earth is named" (Eph 3:14–15). In this perspective, God is not "like" a human father. It would be more proper to say that human fathers are "like" God's perfect and infinite fatherhood, although human fathers reflect God's fatherhood in an imperfect way.

The word *father* as applied to God appears around 250 times in the New Testament, compared to fifteen times in the Old Testament. Christ's great moral discourse, the Sermon on the Mount, presents a way of life that is permeated with the awareness of God's paternal care. Among the many references to God as father contained in this speech is the exhortation to seek perfection through charity toward enemies: "You, therefore, must be perfect, as your heavenly Father is perfect" (Mt 5:48). The prayer and charity of Christ's followers should be directed to the "Father who sees in secret" (Mt 6:4) and who "knows what you need before you ask him" (Mt 6:8). While God's fatherly love was present to some degree in the Old Testament, the New Testament manifests the depths of fatherly love and mercy with a new force and unprecedented closeness to man. We can think, for example, of the image of the merciful father revealed in the parable of the Prodigal Son (Lk 15:11–32).

However, while Christ reveals God's fatherly identity in a new way, he also makes it clear that this fatherhood has a particular and exclusive relation to himself. Jesus distinguishes between his own relationship with the Father and that of his disciples: "my father" (Mt 7:21) in distinction from "your father" (Mt 5:45). In giving his disciples the Lord's Prayer, he teaches them to invoke God the Father in a collective way, as "our Father," but he does not—at least at this particular moment—teach them to individually invoke God as "my father" (Mt 6:9). This usage has a precedent in the Old Testament, which at times makes reference to God acting in a fatherly role toward the entire People of God (see, for example, Dt 32:6).

This usage of the term *father* reflects the profound truth that Christ is the *only* son of the Father. Our own access to God the Father is always by means of a participation in Jesus Christ's unique sonship with the Father. The Gospels offer numerous glimpses of Jesus Christ's intimate relationship with the Father, which reflects the relation between God the Father and God the Son that has existed from all eternity.

At the age of twelve, when Jesus is found by Mary and Joseph in the temple, he responds: "Did you not know that I must be in my Father's house?" (Lk 2:49). Jesus' public ministry begins with the voice of the Father announcing that "this is my beloved Son, with whom I am well pleased" (Mt

3:17). The initial moments of Christ's passion and death also manifest this filial identity. In his impassioned prayer in the Garden of Gethsemane, Jesus prays, "Abba, Father, all things are possible to thee" (Mk 14:36). Mark's version of this scene uses the original Aramaic word *Abba*. This word was associated with the babbling of an infant toward his father, something roughly equivalent to our term "daddy." Such an intimate and direct closeness to God went beyond the usual Jewish sensibility, in which one would not have treated God in such a familiar way.

Christ's words in the Gospel of Matthew give direct expression to his filiation to the Father: "All things have been delivered to me by my Father; and no one knows the Son except the Father, and no one knows the Father except the Son and any one to whom the Son chooses to reveal him" (Mt 11:27). Christ implies here that he alone offers true access to God and God's nature as Father. He, rather than the Law and Prophets which the Chosen People so revered, leads us into the divine life.

John's Gospel gives a particular insight into Jesus' special closeness to the Father. For John, the word *father* has a special meaning, which is different from the human sense of father or the concept of father present in other religions. In contrast to these other notions, in this Gospel the Father is the true God who can only be revealed by the Son, who has shared from all eternity in the divine life: "No one has ever seen God; the only Son, who is in the bosom of the Father, he has made him known" (Jn 1:18).

Beyond simply "closeness" or "intimacy" between the Father and Son, the fourth Gospel presents the relation to the Father as the essential defining feature of the Son's identity. The Son's entire existence depends upon the Father and is oriented toward the Father. As Christ says, "The living Father sent me, and I live because of the Father" (Jn 6:57).

In an eternal act within the Trinity which theologians have described with the term *generation*, the Son receives divine life from the Father. This divine generation is different from any human act of generation, because it occurs within the eternity of God. Because of this order of precedence by which the Father begets the Son—again, within the eternal life of Trinity—the Son can say, "The Father is greater than I" (Jn 14:28). The Son is therefore distinct from the Father in the unity of the one God, while at the same time being equal to the Father, since he is fully God.

Because the Son always exists in this relation to the Father, and in keeping with this principle, the Son's life is fundamentally directed toward the Father. As Christ proclaims, "I have come down from heaven, not to do my own will, but the will of him who sent me" (Jn 6:38). Here we can see how, in the communion of love which unites the Father and the Son, the Son's union with the Father's will takes the form of obedience.

All of these aspects of the relationship between the Father and the Son are specific to these two divine Persons. At the same time, by the will of the Father, the Son offers man the possibility of participating in his own eternal relationship of filiation through the gift of the Holy Spirit. We will now move on to examine this divine filiation of the Christian in more detail.

Grace as Participation in the Filiation of Christ, in the Holy Spirit

The Prologue of John's Gospel states that the Son of God, or the Word, has taken on flesh so as to grant human beings the possibility of becoming children of God (Jn 1:12). As we have seen, no human being can be a "son of God" in the way in which Christ is the eternal Son of the Father. All divine sonship, on the part of believers, is a *sharing* in Jesus' own unique sonship. As Christ states plainly, "No one comes to the Father, but by me" (Jn 14:6).

This possibility of sharing in the Son's own unique filiation was never made explicitly possible during Christ's own lifetime. John reminds us that the Holy Spirit is given as the fruit of Christ's glorification and after Jesus' suffering and death on the Cross (Jn 7:39). The Holy Spirit is thus given to man, as John Paul II commented, "at the price of the Cross which brings about the Redemption." The gift of the Spirit, as the pope went on to comment, brings about a new self-communication of God's own Trinitarian life to man.

As we saw in the last chapter, this presence of the Spirit is the source of a new relationship by which we can enter into personal communion with the three divine Persons. We have examined how the Holy Spirit is the principle of a new life in Christ. This identification with Christ is the basis by which the Christian can invoke God with the intimacy of a Father and live his or her life in relation to God the Father. As Paul notes, the possibility of addressing God as Father is never simply the result of a natural religious instinct: "When we cry, 'Abba! Father!' it is the Spirit himself bearing witness with our spirit that we are children of God" (Rom 8:15–16). By means of the Holy Spirit, the Christian invokes God the Father precisely to the extent that, in a mysterious yet real sense, the believer *is* Christ, through the identification with Christ which takes place in baptism. We are always and only sons and daughters of God through Christ.

This identity of the Christian as a son of God points to the profound transformation that occurs through the sacrament of baptism. Both John and Paul describe this sacrament as a source of new life. The Gospel of John speaks of a new birth (3:5–8), and Paul invites the Romans to reflect on the mysterious identification with Christ's own death and resurrection which occurs in the sacrament: "Do you not know that all of us who have been baptized into Christ Jesus were baptized into his death?" (Rom 6:3). This identification with Christ's death, the apostle continues, leads to a new experience of life, freed from the bonds of sin: "We know that our old self was crucified with him so that the sinful body might be destroyed, and we might no longer be enslaved to sin" (Rom 6:6). Paul speaks of a new life, according to the model of Christ's resurrection, which believers experience even in the present life: "So you also must consider yourselves dead to sin and alive to God in Christ Jesus" (Rom 6:11).

The Fathers of the Church nurtured a sense of wonder before this mystery. The great second-century doctor of the church St. Irenaeus of Lyons expressed amazement at the admirable interchange by which the Son of God, the Word, has taken on a human nature so as to make man an adopted son of God. The Fathers put special emphasis on how this contact with Christ occurs through baptism. In the fourth century, St. Cyril of Jerusalem reminded the newly baptized of this truth, alluding to various texts of the New Testament: "Having been baptized into Christ, and put on Christ, you have been made conformable to the Son of God." As a result, God's plan to raise human beings to the level of divine sonship in light of his only begotten Son, Jesus Christ, has been fulfilled: "For God having foreordained us unto adoption as sons, made us to be conformed to the body of Christ's glory."

Cyril goes on to draw out the consequences of this identification with Christ: "Having therefore become partakers of Christ, you are properly called Christs, and of you God said, Touch not My Christs, or anointed." The Fathers keenly understood that this identification with the Son of God is strengthened through confirmation and actualized in a special way through the Eucharist. As Cyril later comments to the newly baptized, the Body and Blood of Christ is given "that you by partaking of the Body and Blood of Christ, may be made of the same body and the same blood with Him."

In the strict sense, of course, the Christian does not become Christ in the sense of losing his creaturely condition to become Jesus Christ. The Christian becomes Christ in the sense that Christians become "partakers of the divine nature" (2 Pt 1:4). Thomas Aquinas speaks of a "certain participation of natural sonship." *Participation* is an important philosophical concept used by Aquinas, which indicates how someone can have a share in something that belongs to another, without becoming that other.

The human being has a certain participation in God's being and goodness by the very fact of his existence. However, grace involves a participation in God's being which reaches a new level, because it involves a personal relationship of knowledge and love. Such a participation is not possible without grace. Through grace, God allows us to experience a sharing in God the Son's own unique and eternal relationship to God the Father. In this way we can say that we are "introduced" into the life of the Trinity and raised to a new and higher level of existence and action.

Paul describes the specific nature of divine filiation in the believer when he notes that Christians have become sons of God by "adoption as sons" (Gal 4:5). The concept of adoption implies that someone takes on a stranger as a son and an heir out of sheer goodness. With this concept, the apostle expresses the truth that human beings, in their fallen state without grace, are in a state akin to that of strangers in relation to the Trinity. Hence, the notion of adopted sonship reminds us that grace is a gratuitous gift that we, on our own merits, have no right to. Jesus Christ, on the other hand, is Son of God by his very nature.

Divine Filiation in the Spiritual Tradition

As we have seen, the reality of the believer's divine filiation in Christ has a strong basis in the New Testament. This truth was a frequent subject of reflection for the Fathers of the Church, and it had an important place in the teaching of Thomas Aquinas. However, for many centuries, the importance of this truth was not always sufficiently appreciated. As theology became more rational and systematic, there was the risk of losing the sense of mystery which is needed to grasp the reality of divine filiation. The fact of the believer becoming identified with Christ is not easy to explain in a rational way.

Additionally, the development of the modern idea of the person, based on his or her autonomy and freedom, can sometimes make it difficult to appreciate the reality of being a son or daughter of God. In our culture, at times a false and exaggerated vision of freedom can lead us to think of ourselves as existing in absolute independence from God and others. Christ reveals a richer and deeper vision of freedom, which requires a different way of thinking. Grasping this freedom means recognizing that we exist not with absolute independence, but that we exist *in relation*, as God the Son's very being is in relation to God the Father.

Moreover, the development of the theology of grace in the medieval era and afterward led us to the important realization that our own being is elevated by the reality of grace. This was a point that Catholic theology continued to emphasize during the time of the Protestant Reformation. While the believer is indeed raised to a new level of existence through grace, such a perspective did not always give attention to the reality of the filial relationship which is implied by grace.

At the same time, regardless of the importance that theologians have given to this theme, divine filiation has always remained a living and vibrant reality in the Church. From the early centuries, the Church has prayed in a way that reflects the Christian's access to the Father, through the mediation of the Son, and in the power of the Holy Spirit. This tradition is reflected in the current doxology at the end of the Eucharistic prayer: "Through him [Christ], and with him, and in him, O God, almighty Father, in the unity of the Holy Spirit, all glory and honor is yours for ever and ever."

In the nineteenth century, there were signs of renewal in theology and a return to the key sources of Scripture, the Fathers of the Church, and the liturgy. Along with these movements, there was a renewed discovery of the truth of divine filiation. The nineteenth-century German theologian Matthias Josef Scheeben drew renewed attention to the gift of the Holy Spirit as the foundation for divine adoption in Christ. The late nineteenth-century French Carmelite St. Thérèse of Lisieux, honored as a doctor of the church, was instrumental in drawing attention to a spirituality based on the sense of spiritual infancy before God. The Irish monk Bl. Columba Marmion, who lived at the turn of the twentieth century, insisted that the reality of being children of God, through Christ, is central to the Christian life.

St. Josemaría Escrivá incessantly taught that divine filiation offers a firm foundation for the spiritual life. This teaching stemmed above all from his own personal experience, particularly the special contemplative grace which he received on October 16, 1931. While Escrivá was traveling on a streetcar in Madrid, and later walking through the streets of the city, the Holy Spirit enkindled his soul with the tender invocation *Abba, Pater*. This moment of special illumination reminds us how the reality described by Paul—the Holy Spirit who leads the believer to address God the Father with the intimacy of a child of God (Gal 4:6)—can be a lived reality in the life of the Christian.

As the theologians Ernst Burkhart and Javier López point out in their in-depth study of Escrivá's teaching on divine filiation, in this special moment the Holy Spirit led the saint to the keen awareness of being not just like Christ but, in a certain manner, "Christ himself." In continuity with the teaching of the Scriptures and the Church Fathers, the Spanish priest came to recognize the special presence of Christ in the soul of each Christian, identified with the Lord through baptism and confirmation. As a consequence, the disciple is called to live the very life of Christ, conforming his words and actions to the reality present in his soul by grace. Such a life implies a sharing in Christ's priestly sentiments, to the extent that the Christian can be said to "co-redeem" with Christ. This distinctive identity leads the Christian to live in constant communication with the God the Father, God the Son, and God the Holy Spirit, in the midst of those circumstances where God has placed him. There, often in the midst of the most ordinary realities, the Christian is called to sanctify the world and thus build up the Church, Christ's Mystical Body.

Divine Filiation, Belonging to the Church, and Human Fraternity

As Paul affirms, God's plan to raise man to the level of divine sonship is one that concerns all those who are chosen by God, who are thus united as brothers and sisters: "Those whom he foreknew he also predestined to be conformed to the image of his Son, in order that he might be the first-born among many brethren" (Rom 8:29). The incorporation into Christ by baptism unites believers as part of one body of which Christ is the head (1 Cor 12:27); in this way believers form part of the "household of God" (Eph 2:19) and become members of the family of God.

As a result, a Christian cannot separate his identity as a son of God from his status as a son of the Church. As we have seen, the Christian's relationship to God the Father always occurs by means of Christ; we can now add that this relationship to God the Father also entails a relationship of fraternity with all of the brethren whom Christ leads to the same filial relationship.

The Second Vatican Council desired to particularly emphasize this fraternal unity among all those incorporated in Christ. In a world marked by discord and tension, the Council wanted to affirm, using words of the third-century North African bishop St. Cyprian, that the Church can be understood as "a people made one with the unity of the Father, the Son and the Holy Spirit."

This unity within the Church takes on a special character, due to the supernatural bonds created by the believer's incorporation into Christ. However, we should not think of this belonging to the Church in an overly exclusive way, as if divine filiation and unity in Christ were only relevant for members of the Church. The Council's Constitution on the Church states, in its very first paragraph, that "the Church is in Christ like a sacrament or as a sign and instrument both of a very closely knit union with God and of the unity of the whole human race." In other words, the special unity present in the Church is a sign and instrument of the unity which God desires for all of humanity.

A perspective of faith should lead us to appreciate the bonds that unite the entire human race, while at the same time recognizing that faith and baptism are specific factors that distinguish the Christian. As we have seen, the Christian is raised to the level of divine sonship in Christ through the action of grace. Those without baptism are not sons of God in the same sense. Nonetheless, in a different way, we can consider all persons to be children of God, since all are created in God's image and likeness.

Pope Francis has highlighted the fraternal union, or *human fraternity*, which all persons are called to live with one another. For Christians, the awareness of our fellow human beings as brothers and sisters is not simply a truth recognized by human reason, separate from faith. Rather, such human fraternity is a direct consequence of the Christian faith. Francis, citing the words of Pope John Paul II, has noted that "faith has untold power to inspire and sustain our respect for others, for believers come to know that God loves every man and woman with infinite love and 'thereby confers infinite dignity' upon all humanity."

Many persons have not yet experienced the grace of participation in Christ's unique divine filiation, but they are all called to this intimate form of communion with God, and Christ has won for all the grace of salvation. As Francis went on to state, Christians believe that "Christ shed his blood for each of us and that no one is beyond the scope of his universal love." Our theological appreciation of the profound truth of divine filiation should lead us to cherish the exalted condition of living as a child of God, but also move us to a greater concern for all humanity, for whom God wills that same dignity.

CHAPTER 5

Grace as Forgiveness from God: Justification

AS WE SAW IN THE LAST CHAPTER, divine filiation offers a central reference point for understanding the reality of grace. This truth reminds us that grace is a real participation in God the Son's one eternal relationship with God the Father. As we also noted, this truth has not always been a key topic in theology.

In this chapter, we will discuss a topic that has been the subject of much attention over the past centuries: *justification*. This term refers to the moment in which a person passes from the state of sin to a state of friendship with God.

Just as in approaching the truth of grace in general, in studying the topic of justification we need to keep in mind that we are always before a mystery that goes beyond our understanding. It is not easy to comprehend and express how a person can be justified before God. Nonetheless, the New Testament affirms that the justice or "righteousness" of God has been manifested to all who believe in Jesus Christ (Rom 3:22). We can therefore seek to examine this revealed mystery by which we come to receive and participate in God's justice, keeping in mind Catholic tradition as well as the useful insights offered by Protestants.

Justification in the Old Testament

We probably tend to think of *justice* as a legal concept. The Old Testament is in fact filled with a large number of laws which govern the life of the Chosen People. In this context, the law was closely bound together with God's will for his people. The Hebrew word for justice, *sedeq*, conveys a general sense of order; it indicates that which corresponds to a norm.

This connotation of justice was shared by other cultures as well. In the classical Greek world, law was meant to be an expression of a proper order for the person, although this order was seen particularly in reference to the order of man within the larger community. For the people of Israel, justice had the particular sense of a proper ordering of man in relation to God.

In the Old Testament, then, God is the fundamental source of order for all law, both religious law and the other laws that govern the life of society. The divine order offers the unshakeable foundation for all human action, as the Old Testament gives frequent witness. Moses sings to God as "the Rock, his work is perfect; for all his ways are justice. A God of faithfulness and without iniquity, just and right is he" (Dt 32:4).

The Old Testament awareness of justice includes the awareness of God's supremacy, but also looks to the covenant which God formed with his people. Through this covenant, God freely decided to enter into an agreement with his people, which entailed mutual rights and duties. God is just because his actions are always in keeping with the divine order, and also because he remains faithful to the promises he has made to his people. These promises include material prosperity, protection in danger, and also military victory (see, for example, Ex 23:25–29).

In keeping with God's own justice, God acts as ruler and judge of his people. God's justice implies a specific action by which God brings about a just order, through his reward for conduct that is in accord with God's will and punishment for contrary behavior. As the psalmist exclaims: "For the LORD loves justice; he will not forsake his saints. The righteous shall be preserved for ever, but the children of the wicked shall be cut off" (Ps 37:28). God's justice therefore implies the reality of punishment, but this should not lead us to see this justice as a cold and impersonal reality. Justice is above all God's action in favor of his people, and from this perspective, justice and grace can be seen as interchangeable realities, which both express God's loving mercy toward his people: "The LORD is just in all his ways, and kind in all his doings" (Ps 145:17).

This sense of justice, as connected with God's mercy and faithfulness, shows us the fuller meaning of God's justice and the *justification* of man the Old Testament speaks of. God promises the gift of his help so that the Chosen People might receive God's justice and thus be faithful to their covenant. The prophet Hosea announces God's desire to enter into an alliance which is described in terms of a marriage bond, through which the People of God will be confirmed in justice: "I will betroth you to me for ever; I will betroth you to me in righteousness and in justice, in steadfast love, and in mercy" (Hos 2:19).

Through the action of God's justice, we can take on the characteristic of being "just." The Old Testament speaks of just persons as the "righteous" (see, for example, Ps 97:11); this word draws from the same Hebrew root as "justice." The just or righteous man adheres to God, not simply in the sense of an outward completion of God's commandments, but also through an interior submission to God: "His delight is in the law of the LORD, and on his law he meditates day and night" (Ps 1:2).

In the face of the repeated unfaithfulness of the Chosen People, the prophets promise a still greater gift of God, through which God's justice would truly become a reality in the hearts of his people. The prophet Jeremiah announces the new covenant God would make with his people, in the face of

Israel's transgression of the earlier covenant: "I will put my law within them, and I will write it upon their hearts; and I will be their God, and they shall be my people" (Jer 31:33). The future messiah, sent by God, would bring about justice in a definitive way (Is 9:7).

Justification in the New Testament

Jesus Christ takes up and fulfills the Old Testament notion of justice as moral and religious holiness. He announces a righteousness or justice that "exceeds that of the scribes and Pharisees" (Mt 5:20). This justice goes beyond the mere fulfillment of precepts and is an interior reality present in the depths of our being (see, for example, Lk 8:10).

Christ shows us a higher level of justice not simply because he lives the justice of God in an exemplary way, but because Christ himself *is* the justice of God. Paul writes to the Corinthians that God has made Christ Jesus "our wisdom, our righteousness and sanctification and redemption" (1 Cor 1:30). As in the case of the Old Testament Hebrew, the Greek word used here for "righteousness" can also be translated as "justice." Christ himself, true God and true man, reveals that definitive order willed by God to which the scriptural concept of justice points.

John expresses a similar idea in the Prologue of his Gospel, when he states that Christ has surpassed the earlier law: "The law was given through Moses; grace and truth came through Jesus Christ" (Jn 1:17). The words "grace and truth" reflect the Hebrew concepts of *hesed* and *emet,* which were mentioned in chapter two above. *Hesed* is closely connected with the notion of grace, and *emet* means truth or faithfulness. Both of these terms express the justice of God.

Paul's Letter to the Romans is a key scriptural text for understanding how the believer comes to participate in the justice of God manifested in Jesus Christ. In studying the idea of justification present in this epistle, it is important to keep in mind the context. In the letter, Paul explains the message of salvation in Christ Jesus in the face of some teachers who want to oblige Christians to follow the precepts of the Jewish law. Against such teaching, the apostle emphasizes that salvation is a gift God offers to those who have faith, and is not a consequence of following the Old Law: "I am not ashamed of the gospel: it is the power of God for salvation to every one who has faith, to the Jew first and also to the Greek" (Rom 1:16).

The virtue of faith, Paul continues, gives the believer access to the justice or righteousness of God: "For in it [the Gospel] the righteousness of God is revealed through faith for faith; as it is written, 'He who through faith is righteous shall live'" (1:17). Paul quotes the words of the prophet Habakkuk, by which God exhorts his people to trust in his promises in the midst of strife and violence (Hb 1:3, 2:4). For Paul, faith leads to justification from sin, which is the deepest calamity that affects man.

As a backdrop to this teaching on justification, the apostle goes on to describe the sad reality of the "ungodliness and wickedness" of sinful humanity, which incurs "the wrath of God" (Rom 1:18). This state of being under "the power of sin" applies to both Jews and Greeks (Rom 3:9). In the case of the Jews, even the knowledge of God's law only serves to clearly manifest the reality of sin, without giving man the capacity to overcome sin (Rom 3:20).

In the face of the inescapable fact of sin, salvation can only be received as a gift that God offers freely, without any merit on our part: "Since all have sinned and fall short of the glory of God, they are justified by his grace as a gift, through the redemption which is in Christ Jesus" (Rom 3:23–24).

Here, Paul develops an opposition between the carrying out of the Jewish law, on one hand, and the reality of grace on the other. In contrast to the attempt to receive justification by obedience to the law, there is faith, through which the believer is "justified" and is granted "peace with God through our Lord Jesus Christ" (Rom 5:1). By the gift of grace received through faith, we can come to participate in God's justice. As the apostle goes on to assert, "God's love has been poured into our hearts through the Holy Spirit who has been given to us" (Rom 5:5).

While Paul emphasizes that grace is an unmerited gift, this reality should not lead us to think that man remains inactive in the work of justification. The aforementioned words of the prophet Habakkuk, cited by Paul, indicate that the righteous person will "live by faith." The words of Habakkuk recall the Hebrew word for faith, *emunah*, which indicates not simply faith but more broadly an attitude of loyalty and steadfastness. For Paul, this faith involves a commitment by which we give ourselves entirely to God, as shown by Abraham's firm obedience (Rom 4:16–22).

The Letter to the Romans provides a vivid description of the powerful way in which God's action of justification brings about a transformation in the life of the believer. By the "blood" of Christ, Paul states, Christians have been saved from the "wrath of God" which was due to sin (Rom 5:9). This justification is more than simply a legal declaration in which God simply decrees that sin is forgiven. As we have seen, the scriptural notion of justice is deeply bound up with righteousness, which includes the righteousness of God himself as well as the righteousness God asks of us. Thanks to the grace of God, Christians have been set free from sin and are capable of living righteousness through an obedience to God "from the heart" (Rom 6:17). By the action of the Holy Spirit, we can act as children of God who have been "conformed" to the image of Christ (Rom 8:29).

While the state of the justified person involves a genuine liberation from sin and death, this new state of justice does not mean an elimination of sinful tendencies, at least during the believer's earthly life. While he proclaims the authentic liberation brought about by grace, in the Letter to the Romans Paul also recognizes a principle of sin which exists alongside the liberating power of God.

The apostle states that even though Christians' spirits are "alive because of righteousness" through Christ, their "bodies are dead because of sin" (Rom 8:10). In a similar vein, in the Letter to the Galatians he speaks of "the desires of the flesh" which are opposed to "the desires of the Spirit" (5:16–17). Still, even this stark actuality of continued sinful tendencies only serves to accentuate the power of Christ's saving action. The apostle experiences that the "law of the Spirit of life in Christ Jesus" has brought him liberation from "the law of sin and death" (Rom 8:2). While sin and death remain present in the life of the Christian, their dominion over him has been definitively defeated. As the Council of Trent would point out, sin cannot harm those who struggle against it with the grace of God, and the baptized person is given the promise of eternal life.

John also presents the same truth about justification, with a different language. Instead of justification as the initiative of grace, as Paul teaches, John speaks about the "eternal life" which God grants to those who believe (Jn 3:16). For John, as for Paul, this participation in God's own life is a divine initiative and the fruit of God's action within the soul: "No one can come to me unless the Father who sent me draws him" (Jn 6:44).

While John and Paul each refer to the same reality, their respective expressions draw attention to different aspects of the mystery of grace. Although there is much common ground, Paul puts more emphasis on the liberation from sin brought about by grace, while John places more of an accent on how the believer is raised to communion with God. The author of the fourth Gospel describes God's action in the believer as an intimate communion, through which the believer abides in Christ and Christ abides in him (Jn 15:4). Through this communion with Christ, made tangible in the Eucharist, the believer already shares in the "eternal life" which God will fully grant in the final resurrection (Jn 6:40). John is thus able to move beyond the issue of freedom from the Jewish law, and describe justification more positively as an intimate union with the Father, Son, and Holy Spirit (see, for example, Jn 14:23)

Martin Luther's View of Justification

The sixteenth-century German Protestant reformer Martin Luther had a significant impact on the way many Christians understand justification. Luther made this issue the central focus of his efforts to reform the Church.

Luther was educated in the philosophical school known as *nominalism*, which emphasized the absolute power of God and tended to diminish the capacity of human beings to understand God's action. In the area of justification, one version of this school held that justification was simply a declaration by God, which would operate like *nomina* or 'names' in that justification would just be an external sign. That is, God by his power can declare a person to be just without actually bringing about any real change in the person. Other cultural currents of the time also affected Luther's thought. Such influences included an increased emphasis on human autonomy, as well as mystical movements that sought a direct union between God and the soul, thereby doing away with the need for the mediation of the Church.

Beyond this intellectual and spiritual background, Luther's view of justification had profound roots in his own personal religious experience. He felt that the environment at his Augustinian monastery put too much emphasis on the effort to follow the moral law and monastic disciplines. Such an attitude, as he experienced it, was akin to an effort to achieve salvation through carrying out a set of practices.

Luther's "Tower Experience," thought to have occurred around the year 1515, led him to a new insight into the nature of God's justice. Before, he had thought of this justice in terms of God's action of punishing sinners. Through his own intense meditation on Paul's Letter to the Romans, Luther came to appreciate that this justice was not simply a vindictive action, but rather the action of a merciful God who justifies man by faith. This new awareness was a radical turning point. As Luther commented, "All at once I felt that I had been born again and entered into paradise itself through open gates."

From this moment on, Luther had a keen insight into how justification is a free and gratuitous action on God's part, which precedes any effort or merit on our part. This experience led him to assert that justification is completely a divine act. For Luther, even the faith by which we receive justification is not a human act; faith is rather the work of God who acts, as Luther said, *in nobis et sine nobis* (in us and without us). By this faith, the believer abandons himself completely into God's hands and to the divine mercy which has been promised in Christ.

It is important to note that Luther did not try to offer a systematic explanation of the act of faith. Rather, he intended to describe, drawing from his own personal experience, the reality of God's loving action and the way in which we need to put all our confidence in God. Such a submission to God would require not trusting at all in our own efforts. Luther's experience became the basis of a vision of justification which, while having many authentic Christian elements, also contains some aspects—as we shall note—that have appeared incompatible with Catholic teaching. In ecumenical dialogue with Lutherans today, the Catholic Church continues to seek a fully shared understanding of justification with those Christians who are inspired by the teachings of Luther.

Beyond the emphasis on God's gratuitous initiative and man's passivity, Luther's deep sense of the weakness and sinfulness of the human person also affected his notion of what justification entails. In keeping with the nominalist philosophy that had such influence on him, Luther held that justification was an act by which God declares someone to be just, but without bringing about a real change in the person. The justified person would not be held guilty by sin, because of Christ's merits, but the person would continue to have the same evil inclinations as before. As Luther taught, the justified man is "at once a sinner and just" (*simul iustus et peccator*): God declares him to be free of guilt, but he continues to have the same sinfulness as before.

This perspective does not mean that Luther did not perceive the newness of life brought about by Christ, or the importance of good works in the Christian life. For Luther, the new life of grace and good works is the fruit of Christ dwelling in man. In this way, the new life of holiness is really an action of Christ and does not pertain to the believer. Nonetheless, the notion of "at once a sinner and just" seems incompatible with the New Testament's teaching regarding the new life of the Christian, and the Council of Trent would offer an important clarification on the genuine sanctification and inner renewal which takes place in the moment of justification.

Justification According to the Council of Trent

The ecumenical council that gathered in Trent, in the north of present-day Italy, began discussing the issue of justification in June of 1546. After lengthy and intense debate, the Council issued its decree on the topic in January of 1547. The decree offers an explanation of the Church's teaching on justification, inspired by Sacred Scripture, in light of the problems and confusion which had arisen from Luther's teaching.

As a prelude to the teaching on justification, the decree first focuses on man's need for God's gratuitous action to justify him. With numerous references to Scripture, including two allusions to Paul's Letter to the Romans, the Council describes the sorry state of mankind in the state of original sin. All have "lost their innocence" through Adam's sin; they have become "unclean, and (in the words of the Apostle) *by nature children of wrath* . . . slaves of sin and under the power of the devil and death."

Here, like Luther, the Church manifests her awareness of our sinful condition. Luther, however, had emphasized our weakness to the point of teaching that we had become deprived of all capacity for good and that all of our works would be sinful. The Council of Trent corrects such extreme pessimism by affirming that our free will, while weakened and inclined to sin, "was in no way extinct." This statement is significant because it reminds us that while we are in absolute need of God's saving action, there is a still a role for our own free cooperation in the process.

The second and third chapters of the decree describe how justification occurs through the merit of Jesus Christ. On this point, the Council again finds common ground with the teaching of Luther. The German reformer had asserted strongly that man is saved only through Christ. However, Luther had understood this unique mediation of Christ in such a way as to reject all other kinds of mediation, including the intercession of the Blessed Virgin Mary and the saints, as well as the sacramental structure of the Church. In the face of this denial of key truths of the faith, the Council's teaching reminds us that the recognition of Christ's unique mediating role does not exclude other forms of mediation. The decree in fact affirms that the new birth brought about in Christ leads believers to a new communion in the Church, when it states that the Father "has qualified us to share in the inheritance of the saints in light. He has delivered us from the dominion of darkness and transferred us to the kingdom of his beloved Son [see Col 1:12–14]."

The Council goes on to elaborate on some essential aspects of justification. Here, we can see a profound awareness of the priority of God's action, such an important topic for Luther, while at the same time a recognition of how this divine action raises human nature to a new and elevated dignity. As we saw in chapter one, God's grace does not take away human nature but leads this nature to its fulfillment.

The decree states that the action of justification occurs by God's "predisposing grace," through which persons are called to friendship with God "with no existing merits" on their part. The notion of "predisposing grace" clarifies that God's grace is previous to any effort on our part and moves our will to seek justification. At the same time, this action of God counts—the

Council is speaking of the case of adults—on our free response to grace. The decree asserts that believers receive justification "by giving free assent to and co-operating with this same grace." Regarding the need for this free response, the Council Fathers cite the words of the prophet Zechariah: "Return to me, says the LORD of hosts, and I will return to you" (Zec 1:3).

The decree then comments on various aspects of this free response to grace. The person comes to believe in God and in the redemption offered by Christ, which leads him to a hope in God's mercy as well as sorrow for sins and the desire to receive baptism. With these dispositions, a person can receive justification through baptism, or at least through the desire for this sacrament.

The Council Fathers stress that justification is not simply a declaration of God by which we are freed of guilt, but more profoundly an action by which God transforms us from within. Justification, the Council notes, is not simply the forgiveness of sins but "the sanctification and renewal of the inward being" by which "someone from being unjust becomes just, from being an enemy becomes a friend, so that he is an heir *in hope of eternal life* [see Tit 3:7]."

Through this action, God's justice is truly fulfilled within the person, through the charity of God which is poured forth into the believer by the Holy Spirit. As we saw earlier in this chapter, the justice of God can never be reduced to simply a legal concept, but is an expression of the mercy and faithfulness that God shows toward his people. The Council of Trent recognizes that this justice belongs to God, as Luther had so strongly held. The decree affirms that justification is the fruit of the Holy Spirit's action and involves an ingrafting of the believer into Jesus Christ. Nonetheless, in a mysterious way, through the action of grace, this justice becomes an attribute of man. The Council proclaims that through the renewal that takes place in justification, we "are not merely considered to be just but we are truly named and are just [see 1 Jn 3:1]."

From our brief survey in this chapter, we can appreciate why *justification* is such an important term for expressing the meaning of grace. The term reminds us of the fullness of justice and holiness which is present in God. Through his covenant with the Chosen People, and through his alliance with all of humanity in Christ, God desires to make this justice a reality in our hearts. Such justification requires the forgiveness of sin, but such pardon is always connected to a new birth to the life of grace, which affects the whole person. Through the action of the Holy Spirit, God's justice comes to dwell within us and raises us to a new level of justice.

However, the Council of Trent notes that this new birth of justification is simply a beginning of a new principle of life, which is called to grow. Christians are called to cooperate with grace by observing the commandments and by faith acting through works, so that—as the Council observes—they might be further justified. The majesty of God's loving action in justifying believers does not therefore take away human action, but spurs them on to the fullest use of freedom, so as to be identified with Christ in his sufferings and in his glory.

CHAPTER 6

Grace as Interior Transformation

THE GREAT SEVENTEENTH-CENTURY artwork *The Conversion of Saint Paul,* by the Italian painter Caravaggio, provides a powerful insight into the realities that we have been studying. In the painting, the future apostle has fallen to the ground from his horse and covers his eyes before the sudden revelation of divine light. As his companions stand by, in a scene shrouded in darkness, Paul experiences firsthand the newness of the message of Christ. Shortly afterward, as the Acts of the Apostles recounts, he would receive the sacrament of baptism (Acts 9:18)

The image is a moving reminder of the transformation which occurs when the grace of Christ justifies the soul. As we saw in the last chapter, the person becomes—as Paul states—a "new creation" (2 Cor 5:17). His soul experiences, as the Council of Trent solemnly taught, an authentic sanctification and renewal.

However, we might ask: What exactly does it mean to say that we are a "new creation" and that we have been sanctified? In this chapter, will examine these truths in greater detail.

Interior Transformation in Scripture

Paul's Second Letter to the Corinthians, as in the case of other letters of the apostle that we have examined, seeks to explain the distinctiveness of Christianity in comparison with the Old

Law and pagan religion. The new covenant in Christ, as the apostle notes, is written "not with ink but the Spirit of the living God, not on tablets of stone but on tablets of human hearts" (2 Cor 3:3).

In these words, we can see a fulfillment of that interior purification promised by God through the prophet Ezekiel, who describes a "new heart" and "new spirit" which God would place within his people (Ez 36:26). We discussed this passage in chapter three, in reference to the gift of the Holy Spirit. God promises not only that he will give the Holy Spirit, but also that the people themselves will experience a profound purification: "I will sprinkle clean water upon you, and you shall be clean from all your uncleannesses" (Ez 36:25). These words imply that the Chosen People will experience a new state of being, through which they will be empowered to behave in a new manner. In contrast with the past, as a result of this sanctifying action of God, the people will be able to walk in God's statutes and be careful to observe his ordinances (Ez 36:27). The gift of the Spirit is connected with the capacity to rise up from the grave (Ez 37:12–14).

These texts point to the way God's justifying action gives rise to a new state within the believer. When Paul speaks of the new creation, the word *new* does not simply mean "that which was not there before." The Greek word for *new* used by Paul rather implies that the Christian is new in nature and superior to that which came before. The term is used in Scripture to imply the definitive fulfillment which will come at the end of time, as in the "new heaven" and "new earth" spoken of in the Book of Revelation (21:1). The Christian, in the present life, already shares in this fulfillment.

The content of this "newness" is a reconciliation with God, which has taken the place of the reality of sin that reigned before Christ. This state of man, prior to the coming of Christ, is the "old nature" (Eph 4:22), which indicates the sinful tendencies of man. "Old" also indicates the "old covenant" (2 Cor 3:14), that is, the covenant God made with Moses. This "old covenant," as Paul indicates, could not lead the Chosen People to true intimacy with God. Without Christ, there is a hardening of heart and a "veil" that prevents the people from "beholding the glory of the Lord" (2 Cor 3:14–15; 3:18). Through the gift of the Spirit, Christians can come to perceive this glory and as a result experience an inner transformation. They "are being changed into [the Lord's] likeness from one degree of glory to another" (2 Cor 3:18).

Another important term used by Paul to describe the new state of the Christian is *regeneration*. This word could signify a "return to existence" or a "renewal to higher existence." For the Jews, this term came to be seen particularly in relation to God's action in giving life to his people. The first-century Jewish philosopher Philo used the word to describe how God reconstituted the world after the flood. For Jews at the time of Christ, this word was associated with the future new existence which God would grant to his people, in which righteousness would dwell. This future existence would not simply be a new "life," but would also involve a moral renewal.

The Gospel of Matthew uses the Greek word for "regeneration" to indicate the "new world" (Mt 19:28) which will come when Christ reigns in glory. Paul, however, indicates that this regeneration has already occurred in the gift of justification. In the Letter to Titus, he notes that Christians have been saved, not by any merit but by God's mercy, "by the washing of regeneration and renewal in the Holy Spirit, which he poured out upon us richly through Jesus Christ our Savior" (Ti 3:5–6). In connection with this action of regeneration, Paul speaks once more of an inner transformation which is also evident in outward behavior. Before God's justifying action, the apostle notes, "we ourselves were once foolish, disobedient, led astray, slaves to various passions and pleasures" (Ti 3:3).

Finally, we can make mention of one more important New Testament term for expressing the new state of the believer after justification: *koinonia* or "participation." This word is connected with the idea of commonality, in the sense of having common ownership over something. *Koinonia* indicates a participation in which one shares something with another. In Greek, the term could sometimes be used to indicate that one shares in something he does not possess. The word did not simply mean the sharing of certain goods but also signified a close fellowship between the two parties.

Koinonia was often used in the Greek world to describe man in relation to God. However, the word had more of a connotation of union with God, in the sense that the person would actually become a god. In this way, the distinction between God and man was blurred.

Understandably, given this context, the Greek Old Testament refrained from using *koinonia* to express the relationship of the Israelite to God. The Jewish people recognized that their relationship to God was completely different from that of the pagans with their gods. The Chosen People recognized their dependence upon God and their need to trust in him. In keeping with this sense of reverence and respect, they would not have considered themselves to be in fellowship or companionship with God.

This background can help us to appreciate the radical truth conveyed by the word *koinonia* as used in the New Testament. Through Christ and the Holy Spirit, the believer is truly brought into fellowship with God, but without confusing the distinction between the creature and the Creator. As we discussed in chapter four, the Second Letter of Peter reminds Christians that they have been freed from worldly corruption and "become partakers [Greek *koinonoi*] of the divine nature" (2 Pt 1:4).

The term *koinonia* therefore reminds us of the radical closeness to God that has come about through justification. Believers are "heirs" (Rom 8:17) to eternal life: through their identification with Christ, they can be said to have a "right" to communion with God as if somehow this communion with God was their property. Such is the intimate sharing in God's life granted to believers in Christ.

For Paul, Jesus Christ is the indispensable foundation for the very possibility of *koinonia* with God. The apostle, in fact, never uses this term to speak directly of participation in God. Rather, fellowship with God is always mediated by the Person of Jesus Christ as well as by the Holy Spirit. Paul reminds the Corinthians that God is the one "by whom you were called into the fellowship of his Son, Jesus Christ our Lord" (1 Cor 1:9). The incorporation into Christ's death and resurrection through baptism forms the basis of the Christian's participation in the life of God, as we saw in chapter four (Rom 6:4). This sharing in the divine life takes on a special closeness in the Eucharist: "The cup of blessing which we bless, is it not a participation [*koinonia*] in the blood of Christ?" (1 Cor 10:16).

The Christian's close intimacy with Christ, in turn, forms the basis of the intimate fellowship which is characteristic of the Church. John, using the same Greek term, expresses the desire to his audience that "you may have fellowship with us," while at the same time he recognizes the basis of such communion: "Our fellowship is with the Father and with his Son Jesus Christ" (1 Jn 1:3).

This brief overview of some words related to justification can allow us to appreciate some key points about the meaning of the transformation which occurs through grace. The Christian is a new creation through the new presence of an intimate and personal relationship with God. While grace always implies this relationship, at the same time this relationship gives rise to a new condition within the redeemed person himself. There is a stable condition or *state* through which the person comes to live in a new intimacy with God and in a new level of holiness. The Fathers of the Church meditated with wonder at this mystery, and later theologians would offer a more systematic explanation.

The Reflection on Grace during the Scholastic Period

Scholasticism, or the philosophy of the "schools," was characterized by the attempt to apply the powers of reason to comprehend the whole of reality, including the Christian faith. An important stage in this process was the effort to bring together the philosophy of Aristotle and Christianity. A number of thinkers sought to understand the truths of grace from this philosophical perspective.

Such an approach led to certain difficulties and debates. Aristotle understood virtue as an "excellence" or perfection that allows a person to engage in virtuous activity, which is the highest activity of man. Moral virtue, for this famed Greek philosopher, is a stable disposition that allows the person to be guided by reason. A virtue is something that is a characteristic of a person, rather than an action. For example, a person with the virtue of fortitude has a disposition to be courageous before difficulties. Nonetheless, having this virtue would be different from an action that involved fortitude—for example, the construction of a house.

Still, while virtues are qualities of a person, these qualities are formed from action. To use the example just mentioned, I might gain the virtue of fortitude, which is a stable quality, precisely through the *action* of building a house. From the experience of building that house, I would have a greater readiness to face the future difficulties which will come from building additional houses: getting the materials together, laying the foundation, and so on.

Christian thinkers, influenced by Plato and Aristotle, examined how the reality of grace gives rise to certain virtues or dispositions to the good within the person. As we have seen in this chapter, Sacred Scripture reminds us that God's action of justification gives rise to a new state within the person. In other words, justification is an action of God, but it has a real *effect* within the person which is distinct from God himself. This divine action gives rise to a "new heart and new spirit," and the believer is a "new creation."

St. Anselm, the Italian Benedictine monk and doctor of the church who lived at the turn of the twelfth century, was one of the first theologians to consider how grace might give rise to a specific *virtue* or stable habit in the person. Inspired by the thought of Augustine, Anselm held that grace gives rise to a *rectitude* within the will and in action. This rectitude is similar to human virtue, in that it gives the person a disposition to carry out the good. But it is also different from virtue, in that rectitude is a gift of God's grace, and if a person loses this grace, he would lose this rectitude.

Anselm's position brings up a dilemma the Scholastic theologians faced when they approached the idea of virtues in relation to grace. Are the virtues that come with grace true virtues, which perfect the person, or are they simply gifts of God? Peter Abelard, an influential twelfth-century Scholastic thinker, proposed another approach to this question. Abelard, in keeping with Aristotle's approach, put more emphasis on virtue as a stable quality within the soul. According to his view, grace would mean that the believer experiences an energy and power in his own soul, in such a way that there would not be a need for specific help from God—actual grace—to carry out a good action.

Abelard desired to emphasize the self-reliance that God wanted to give to human beings. However, his position did not account for the truth that grace, which we know as actual grace, is indeed needed for a truly good action. Nonetheless, he and other thinkers of this period helped to pave the way for a better understanding of a *theological virtue*. Theological virtues are like ordinary human virtues in that they are qualities which are stable habits within the person. At the same time, they are unlike the human virtues in that they are supernatural gifts of God. The practice of theological virtues, furthermore, requires the continual assistance of God's grace.

An important step in the Scholastic reflection on grace was the debate over Peter Lombard's interpretation of the Letter to the Romans 5:5: "God's love has been poured into our hearts through the Holy Spirit who has been given to us." As we discussed in chapter 3, Lombard held that this passage implies that the Holy Spirit is literally the love that has been poured into our hearts. In this view, Lombard sought to be faithful to Augustine and Augustine's appreciation that God's grace is necessary for any action.

However, Lombard's position does not fully appreciate the way in which the believer is truly transformed by grace. In this regard, his view is not that of Augustine. In some of

Augustine's writings, due to the specific context in which he was writing, Augustine put particular emphasis on how God is the one at work in justification. Nonetheless, he also had a deep awareness that this grace brings about a transformation of human nature. The North African bishop understood Paul's words in Romans 5:5 as an affirmation of the gift of love which God makes to us, but also as a statement of the way God gives us a new capacity to love. As Augustine commented, regarding this text of Paul: "Now '*the love of God*' is said to be shed abroad in our hearts, not because He loves us, but because He makes us lovers of Himself."

In contrast to this view of Augustine, Lombard's position—that the Holy Spirit is the one who loves when the Christian loves—does not fully fathom the way the Christian has been raised up to the capacity of love by grace. In fact, Lombard's view led a number of medieval authors to reflect on what exactly the transformation of the believer involves. Theologians came to better comprehend how God's justifying action gives rise to a stable condition or a *state* of the soul.

This abiding state of the soul is distinct from a virtue, which is an *operative* habit that disposes us to "operate" or to act in a morally upright way. Grace, as medieval theologians came to realize, does not simply give the Christian the disposition to act in a certain way. Rather, grace is—as one asserted—an *entitative* habit, which means that it gives the believer a new manner of being.

Perhaps such reflections might seem a bit philosophical and not very relevant to the way we think about grace. Certainly, not all of the distinctions of medieval theologians form part of the Church's doctrine. Still, we can appreciate the Scholastic reflection as a way of expressing the essential truth, revealed by Scripture, that the believer is truly born again and becomes a new creation. In keeping with this vision, the *Catechism of the Catholic Church* emphasizes the way grace leads to the presence of a new condition in the soul: "Sanctifying grace is an habitual gift, a stable and supernatural disposition that perfects the soul itself to enable it to live with God, to act by his love." The *Catechism* here affirms that grace perfects the soul as a whole, giving it a stable disposition "to live and act in keeping with God's call." In other words, the new *state* of grace leads to certain specific habits, the *theological virtues*, by which the believer lives out his closeness to God.

In the case of human virtues, the presence of virtue does not automatically lead to virtuous action. A person might be filled with fortitude, yet perhaps at a given moment he might lack strength to live this virtue in the face of a certain challenge. The theological virtues, like the human virtues, need to be put into practice, but in the case of theological virtues there is a need for additional help from God.

The reality of freedom entails that the believer also has the possibility of rejecting God through mortal sin. Such sin occurs when a person turns away from God in a serious matter, with full knowledge and deliberate consent. In such a case, the believer loses that stable state of grace he had previously enjoyed. The person becomes prey to disordered passions and the temptations of the devil. Nonetheless, the awareness of the possibility of mortal sin should never lead us to discouragement. God continues to offer sinners the grace of repentance. Through contrition and the sacrament of reconciliation, the sinner can receive once more the merits of Christ and recover the state of grace, thus renewing his friendship with God and communion with the Church.

After speaking of the stable disposition to live with God, known as *habitual* grace, the *Catechism* makes reference to actual graces, which are "at the beginning of conversion or in the course of the work of sanctification." This distinction reminds us that grace brings out a true transformation in the believer, through which he is inclined to love God, and yet at the same time the believer remains constantly in need of God's help.

Thomas Aquinas on Grace

We have already had several occasions to refer to Thomas Aquinas' insights regarding grace. In his great work *Summa Theologiae*, this illustrious doctor of the church has a series of questions dedicated to the topic of grace. These questions present a profound synthesis of the Church's thinking with regard to the mystery of grace.

Significantly, Aquinas places this extended section on grace within the part of the *Summa* dedicated to human moral action. This placement reminds us that grace is a reality which, while it comes from God, acts within human nature. The Angelic Doctor—as Aquinas is known—recognizes that man, and especially man in the state of original sin, needs grace in order to act in a way that is genuinely good.

While grace indicates a special help given by God, Aquinas' examination of grace makes clear that grace is a reality which is present within us. That is, grace is not simply an action from the "outside," in the way a puppeteer might operate a puppet. Rather, as the Dominican theologian points out, "when a man is said to have the grace of God, there is signified something bestowed on man by God," even though the word *grace* can sometimes be used in Scripture to refer to God himself.

Aquinas understands grace to be a "quality" or a characteristic which is present in the very essence of the soul of the believer, and which gives him a new and supernatural way of being. This new state is not simply the presence of the virtues of faith, hope, or love, which allow us to *act* in a supernatural way. Previous to this capacity for *acting*, God elevates our *being* to a new supernatural mode of existing. This new state affects the entire person and is a participation in the divine life. As a result, as Aquinas points out, God sees the creature in a different way. The creature is now loved by God with the same love which God has for the only true object of his love, which is God himself. The person is now in a new state that is, as the Angelic Doctor notes, "pleasing to God."

As a result of this new supernatural way of existing, the person now has an inclination, *within himself*, toward God. As the great Dominican doctor asserts, through the gift of grace God grants to us "certain forms and powers, which are the principles of acts, in order that they may of themselves be inclined to these movements." In this way, as he goes on to comment, supernatural acts become "natural" to us: "thus the movements whereby they are moved by God become natural and easy to creatures, according to Wisdom 8:1: 'she . . . ordereth all things sweetly.'" The person, raised to a new identity as a son of God by grace, now has an inner impulse to live in communion with God. As we noted in chapter two, Aquinas described this grace that acts in us as "created grace," not because grace is something "created," but because we are given a new identity through it.

Other Christian communities, such as the Orthodox and Lutheran communities, have had a hard time accepting the notion of habitual or sanctifying grace, which has such importance in Catholic theology. Some have been led to the idea that Catholics think of grace as somehow a "thing," which the believer takes possession of, and which gets in the way of God's action. However, Catholic theology has traditionally seen that grace is not a "thing" but rather a "habit," which is a quality or a "way of being" rather than a being itself. Grace is a characteristic of the person, which gives the person a new way of being, but it does not imply that a new "thing" comes to the person. Rather, the human being, while remaining a human being, comes to be a human being in a new and supernatural way.

In speaking about or explaining the reality of grace today, often it will not be necessary to use all of the philosophical and theological terms used by the Scholastics. Still, as we have emphasized in this chapter, these terms fundamentally describe an important reality, expressed in Scripture: the human person and his nature are truly transformed and raised to a new level of being. This transformation is always the fruit of God's work and is ordered to God, but it is also something distinct from God, because it affects our identity. As the *Catechism of the Council of Trent* stated, grace is a quality which "inheres in the soul"; it is, "as it were, a brilliant light that effaces all those stains which obscure the lustre of the soul, investing it with increased brightness and beauty." The believer who experiences the gift of justification truly becomes, as Paul so clearly affirms, "a new creation" (2 Cor 5:17).

Grace, Virtues, and Gifts of the Holy Spirit

We have seen how sanctifying grace leads to a new state that affects the person in his entirety. This state, as we have also noted, is distinct from the virtues but also gives rise to the theological virtues, by which man has the capacity to act in a new way. This capacity might not always be put into practice, for example in the case of infants. Infants receive what medieval theologians called the "habit" of the virtues. This means that they have received the grace through which they are empowered to live the virtues, even if they are not yet able to exercise these virtues through actions.

The three theological virtues of faith, hope, and love allow us to live in communion with God. In these virtues, the action of grace elevates our ordinary human capacities. Faith is traditionally associated with the intellect, in that it leads the believer to accept God's revelation as true. Hope, on the other hand, perfects the will so that it might trust God in the face of the difficulties the believer encounters in reaching eternal life. Love strengthens the will, but in a different way, so that it might be united to God, the perfect good, and to others out of love for God.

Aquinas, with many others in the Catholic tradition, holds that along with the theological virtues, God also grants to the Christian a special capacity to live the moral virtues of prudence, justice, fortitude, and temperance. These virtues, considered as a special gift of God through grace, are known as the *infused moral virtues.*

The moral virtues, unlike the theological virtues, are virtues that do not necessarily require grace and do not necessarily involve a participation in the divine life. The Greek philosophers Plato and Aristotle appreciated them as essential virtues for the life of the individual as well as society. Grace, as we have seen, brings about a transformation of the entire person. In keeping with this truth, a Christian perspective allows us to see these noble human qualities in a new, supernatural perspective informed by charity. Furthermore, the grace of God gives a special strength to the Christian, so as to overcome the sinful tendencies which obstruct the practice of virtue. Among many examples, we can think of the recently canonized Dutch saint, Titus Brandsma. Brandsma was a Carmelite priest and journalist who lived exceptional fortitude in speaking the truth in the face of Nazi persecution.

Finally, our description of the new reality produced by sanctifying grace would not be complete without reference to the *gifts of the Holy Spirit*. While the virtues perfect the human capacities of the person, the gifts of the Holy Spirit dispose the Christian to be moved by God. Thomas Aquinas, who was instrumental in developing our current conception of the seven gifts, recognized that the seven gifts fill a need in our soul, in light of the reality of sanctifying grace. While grace raises up our capacity to a participation in the divine life, this contact with the divine life requires some additional habits, given by God, so that we can act in a supernatural way.

Based on an ancient Greek translation of Isaiah 11:1–3, which speaks of the different ways in which the Spirit of the Lord will rest on the messiah, the Christian tradition has enumerated seven gifts of the Holy Spirit. Each one, in a different way, equips us to act according to a supernatural instinct that goes beyond our natural capacities.

The first four gifts relate in a particular way to the intellect. *Wisdom* allows the Christian to perceive God as the cause and end of all things. *Understanding* grants deeper insight into the truths of the Faith. *Counsel* provides discernment on how to order created things for the glory of God and according to God's loving plan. *Knowledge* helps Christ's disciples to perceive the practical way of doing God's will in each moment. The other three gifts relate to the will. The gift of *fortitude* bestows a new force to seek the difficult good, which strengthens the infused moral virtue of fortitude. *Piety* leads the Christian to relate to God in accord with his identity as a son of God. Finally, the *fear of the Lord* brings a sense of reverence for God, by which we also come to detest sin.

The presence of the gifts in the life of the Christian are a powerful reminder of the way in which the Christian is truly reborn and transformed, by grace, to live the supernatural life of divine sonship. Raised to communion with the divine life, by these gifts the believer learns—as Pope Francis has commented—"to see with God's eyes, to feel with God's heart, to speak with God's words."

CHAPTER 7

Man's Need for Grace

IN PREVIOUS CHAPTERS, we have looked at different ways in which grace acts in the person: freeing him from sin, leading him to the identity of a son of God, raising his whole being to a new supernatural level. Our focus has been on grace as an action of God which, without any merit on our part, grants us a profound new identity.

In all of these actions of God, as we have seen, the human person does not remain inactive. In this chapter and the next, we will look more closely at the human being's own powers in relation to grace. The relationship between God's gift of grace and our free response is a great mystery, and one that has been a source of intense debate over the centuries. Nonetheless, this topic is a crucial one for theology and the Christian life. In this chapter, we will study our need for grace.

Scriptural Testimony on the Need for Grace

Today, at a time in which human effort and ingenuity have led to progress in so many areas of human life, we can find it difficult to accept that we are in need of grace. At the same time, along with these advances we see all too many signs of the human capacity for evil. The Second Vatican Council describes the world as "the theater of man's history, and the heir of his energies, his tragedies and his triumphs; that world which the Christian sees as created and sustained by its Maker's love, fallen indeed into the bondage of sin, yet emancipated now by Christ." The Church sees human action in the world with all its capacity for greatness, and yet remains aware of the sad possibility of sin. As the Council went on to note, when man looks into his heart, he "finds that he has inclinations toward evil too, and is engulfed by manifold ills which cannot come from his good Creator."

Sacred Scripture presents to us a vivid portrait of our immense dignity as a being created in the image and likeness of God. Divine revelation also shows us the sad reality of sin, which deeply affects humanity and also the life of the Chosen People. Early in the Book of Genesis, as this tragic history of man's "wickedness" unfolds, the sacred writer comments that "the LORD was sorry that he had made man on the earth, and it grieved him to his heart" (Gn 6:6).

Confronting the continual reality of man's unfaithfulness, the prophets recognized that a divine gift would be needed for the Chosen People to fully live their covenant with God. The people realized that God himself must be the one to help them come back to God after their sin. They cry out: "Restore us to thyself, O LORD, that we may be restored!" (Lam 5:21) Through the prophet Jeremiah, God announces: "I will put my law within them, and I will write it upon their hearts" (Jer 31:33).

From these and other passages, we can discern that we are in need of a special help of God, in addition to simply knowing the law, in order to carry out God's will. The awareness of this truth is strengthened by the revelation brought about in Jesus Christ. The New Testament, as we have seen, is a constant witness to the reality of God's grace. These books of Scripture also show us how deeply we are in need of this gift. In fact, only in the New Testament does the true reality of our sinfulness and need for grace come to be fully expressed. At the Last Supper, on the eve of his self-giving on the Cross,

Christ tells the apostles that the Holy Spirit "will convince the world of sin and of righteousness and of judgment" (Jn 16:8).

As John Paul II comments, the very reality of original sin is a lack of truthfulness and a rejection of God's love. Because of this condition, we are incapable of being aware of the full reality of sin, and we need the Holy Spirit to "convince" us of this truth. In other words, we need grace in order to recognize our own need for grace. We are especially prone to deny this reality, precisely because of the pride caused by our sinful condition.

Our blindness to sin, due to our fallen state, does not mean that we are not aware of sin at all. Sin is in fact a conscious turning away from God. Paul, describing this sinful condition which he himself experiences, on one hand "delight[s] in the law of God, in my inmost self" (Rom 7:22). In the context, we can understand that Paul here refers to an awareness of sin that is distinct from grace. Along with this awareness, Paul goes on to comment, "I see in my members another law at war with the law of my mind and making me captive to the law of sin which dwells in my members" (7:23). Many scriptural commentators understand this "I" as not simply referring to Paul himself, but to a common experience of all who must face the conflict between the Law of Moses and the reality of their sinfulness. These words can therefore help us to see the way in which sinfulness comes to dominate us in spite of our capacity to know the good.

Moved by his awareness of the meaning of redemption in Christ, Paul shows an understanding of our sinful condition which goes beyond that present in the Old Testament, and which helps us to better understand our constant need for grace. While the Old Testament generally understands sin to be an act by which man rejects God, for Paul sin is a *state* which affects the human race. As a result, man in his sinful state does not fully have the freedom to follow God's will, even if to some degree he can know this will.

The coming of Christ, and in particular his passion, death, and resurrection, is the only way this sinful state can be overcome. As Paul notes in the Letter to the Romans, only through the "law of the Spirit of life in Christ Jesus," that is, through the action of the Holy Spirit which communicates Christ's salvation, can we be freed from captivity to the law of sin (Rom 8:2).

John's Gospel suggests the same truth of our dependence on Christ, by means of the image of Christ as the true vine and Christ's followers as branches. The image of the vineyard was familiar in the Old Testament and evokes the fruits of righteousness which God expects of his people (Is 5:1–7). Christ affirms that union with him, the true vine, is the precondition for bearing fruit: "Apart from me you can do nothing" (Jn 15:5). Here, we see clearly that union with Christ is the basis for carrying out actions which are truly good, in the sense of being fully pleasing to God (Jn 15:7–8).

The First Letter of John depicts the Christian's continual reliance on Christ in more detail. The beloved disciple states that "no one born of God commits sin; for God's nature abides in him, and he cannot sin because he is born of God" (1 Jn 3:9). The new birth of the Christian through baptism means that "God's nature abides in him," and through this sharing in the divine life he has a new capacity to triumph over sin.

These images from the writings of Paul and John present a vivid image of the way in which God's action is continually at work in the ordinary actions of the Christian. They remind us that the action of grace, which leads the believer to a participation in the unique divine filiation of God the Son, leads to a way of acting that breaks the limits of our sinful condition and makes our actions pleasing to God.

This need for God's help is not always evident to reason, even that of the believer, since grace works in a silent way in the depths of our soul. Nonetheless, Paul reminds the Philippians that God is at work at every stage of the Christian's life. God is the one who began "a good work in you," through the Christian's initial incorporation into Christ, and God is furthermore the one who will "bring . . . to completion" this same work at the time of Christ's Second Coming (Phil 1:6). The source of this good, as the apostle makes clear, is Christ. The "fruits of righteousness," which should abound in the life of the Christian, "come through Jesus Christ, to the glory and praise of God" (Phil 1:11).

Paul, in the same letter, goes on to describe the way all Christian behavior draws from faith and adoration of Christ. In this perspective, God is continually present, acting in the interior of the believer: "God is at work in you, both to will and to work for his good pleasure" (Phil 2:13).

In light of this scriptural overview, we can perceive the way in which we are absolutely in need of the help of God, offered through Christ, in order to surmount the reality of our sinful condition and carry out the good. However, we have also seen that the awareness of our need for God's help is itself a reality of faith which Christ reveals. As a result, in our current condition, we easily run the risk of losing sight of this supernatural truth, as we shall see.

Pelagianism

The scriptural truths we have studied in this chapter became particularly relevant in light of the spread of the teaching of

Pelagius. Not much is known about him. He arrived in Rome, from Britain, toward the end of the fourth century. He lived a celibate life and was deeply committed to the practice of virtue. He was also a skilled teacher and writer who attracted many followers.

Pelagius felt deeply that man can and should achieve moral perfection. He was firmly convinced that people, on the strength of their own nature, could reach such excellence. He distinguished between three aspects in this process: the ability to carry out an action, the willing of an action, and the actual carrying out of an action. In his view, God has given to us the ability to do good, but we ourselves are the ones responsible for the willing and the carrying out of righteous deeds.

Pelagius wanted his fellow men to realize what they were capable of doing good through their own efforts. He put great emphasis, like many persons today, on our freedom of choice. Pelagius did recognize that we could misuse this freedom through sin. Still, he felt that human nature could not remain wounded by sin, even in the case of Adam and Eve.

Certainly, Pelagius' aims were praiseworthy. He stressed the goodness of creation and the reality of our freedom. At the same time, his notion of virtue reflects more of a pagan than a Christian vision. According to such a perspective, the virtues are the result of purely human effort. This emphasis on achieving perfection through willpower had a great attraction for many in Rome. Many at the time had become Christians as a matter of social convention and were still attached to pagan ideals.

In pursuing their noble ideals, Pelagius and his followers embraced an ethos of self-improvement that, while having an appearance of rationality, ignored the revealed truth of Scripture. Pelagius would not accept that our own power of self-improvement was lacking, and as a consequence he rejected the idea of original sin. He was repulsed by the notion that we would need "special help," which he saw as a kind of favoritism, to carry out God's will.

Celestius, one of Pelagius' most devoted followers, was the instigator of the controversy in which Augustine would become involved. While passing through the North African city of Carthage, Celestius engaged in debate regarding the question of the origin of the soul and how each human being might be held responsible for the sin of Adam. In this context, this disciple of Pelagius attacked the traditional practice, present from apostolic times, of baptizing infants for the forgiveness of sins. At the time, many in the North African Church subscribed to the teaching of St. Cyprian, according to which the baptism of infants took place for the sin of Adam.

Cyprian's teaching suggested that Adam's sin was the reason for the reality of death, as well as the cause of an inclination to sin in all of Adam's descendants. Celestius, to the contrary, subscribed to the position that death is natural to man, and not a consequence of Adam's sin. We would be punished only for our own individual sins. As a result, baptism is not necessary for the remission of sins, but rather for entering into the kingdom of God. Celestius' views aroused the firm opposition and condemnation of the bishops of Carthage.

Pelagius and his followers had a severely diminished notion of grace. They held—at least initially—that grace does not act within the soul but rather is an external divine help. Such helps would include the example of Christ and the saints, as well as the orientation offered by the moral law. These aids make living the commandments easier but are not necessary for us to act well.

In the face of condemnations of his teaching, Pelagius admitted that a kind of interior grace could work within us.

Such grace would operate, for example, through listening to sermons or reading the Bible. These actions can cause an illumination in the mind which would make it easier to carry out good works, by giving us a greater knowledge of the good. However, for Pelagius, the action of grace does not extend to the gift of charity, which strengthens the will.

Pelagius and his followers thus accepted a certain notion of grace, but not a grace that truly transforms us. When it came to fulfilling the commands, we would count on the strength of our own nature and would not need the help offered by God.

Augustine's Response to Pelagian Teaching

At the time, Augustine was the bishop of Hippo, a city which, like Carthage, was located in central North Africa. His friend Marcellinus informed him of the Pelagian controversy and asked him to intervene. As Augustine recounts in his autobiography, *The Confessions*, he himself had come to experience firsthand his own incapacity to carry out the good and the transforming power of grace. Augustine quickly grasped, with more clarity than his contemporaries, that the views of Pelagius were a profound betrayal of the Christian faith. The bishop of Hippo realized that Pelagius did not truly comprehend the sinful condition of man before God, as revealed in Scripture. As a result, Pelagius lacked an awareness of the true nature of salvation in Christ.

The errors of Pelagius and his followers would provide an opportunity for Augustine to clarify some essential points regarding the revealed truth about grace and about our need for this special help from God. The bishop of Hippo's deep awareness of our tendency to sin should not be seen as the consequence of a pessimistic attitude toward humanity. In fact, it was precisely his understanding of our sinfulness that led Augustine to realize that the Church's mission is oriented toward everyone. While Pelagianism reached out to those select few who could live the moral law to a high degree of perfection, Augustine recognized that the Church exists for the express purpose of bringing God's grace to the entire human race, with all of its moral weaknesses.

Through his analysis of Pelagius' views and in light of the truths conveyed in Sacred Scripture, Augustine was the first person to develop the doctrine of original sin. According to this doctrine, as a result of Adam's sin the human being lives in a radical *state* of sin and all of humanity is born with *concupiscence*, or an inclination toward sin. On our own, we are unable to overcome this situation. Therefore, we are in absolute need of the help of grace acting within our soul.

We should not understand Augustine's position here to mean that we are completely lacking all capacity for goodness. Against the Manicheans, who held that God was the cause of evil, Augustine had in fact emphasized the reality of free will. He had realized that man, even in his present condition marked by sin, still has a *desire* (and the capacity) to do the good. However, only with the help of grace can this desire turn into the actual *realization* of the good.

The gift of grace, then, is needed to overcome our fallen condition. As we saw in the last chapter, in light of Paul's affirmation in Romans 5:5, Augustine recognizes that the love of God has been poured out into the soul of the Christian through the Holy Spirit. This gift of grace is a completely free gift, which we can do nothing to merit. This illustrious doctor of the church cites the practice of infant baptism as a sign of the gratuitousness of grace and a reminder that original sin is present in every unbaptized person.

According to Augustine, grace overcomes the inclination to sin by introducing what the bishop of Hippo termed a *delectatio victrix*, literally a "victorious pleasure." With this phrase, Augustine sought to describe the way God leads the person to the true good by means of grace. God accomplishes this, without infringing upon our freedom, by presenting to us the attractiveness of the good. Augustine here speaks of a theological reality that reflects his own conversion, in which he recognized God's grace leading him out of captivity to sin and toward a passionate love for God. As he recounts in *The Confessions*, describing his liberation from the chains of sin, "What at one time I feared to lose, it was now a joy to me to put away." God himself, Augustine acknowledges, had become the "true and highest sweetness."

Augustine's writings did not intend to provide a systematic analysis of the state of grace, as the Scholastic theologians would later do. The bishop of Hippo, like many of the Fathers of the Church, prefers the language of *divinization*, which draws attention to the way in which God raises us up to the divine life. In this perspective, Augustine continually emphasizes the way we depend on God's holiness. In addition to the grace of justification, Augustine recognizes the need for the continual help of grace, later known by theologians as *actual grace*. By means of actual grace, God not only inclines the soul toward the good act but also brings about, without fail, the consent of the will to this good act. Because this grace has the power to bring about the good act—once again, without violating our freedom, because the will becomes enamored of the good—this grace is known as *efficacious grace*.

In his writings, Augustine often accentuates that grace is a supernatural and gratuitous gift of God, which is distinct from our free will. As a result, sometimes these writings can give the impression that God's grace completely overcomes human freedom. It is important to keep in mind that Augustine's teachings against Pelagianism occurred in a very different context from his earlier writings against the Manicheans. In the Pelagian controversy, Augustine was less focused on philosophy and more attentive to the theological truth of our utter helplessness without grace.

Still, Augustine was keenly aware that we remain free before the action of grace. In fact, the powerful action of God within the soul, far from taking away our freedom, gives us the truest freedom. As the historian and expert on Augustine Peter Brown points out, for Augustine freedom "cannot be reduced to a sense of choice: it is a freedom to act fully."

Far from being reduced, the free will achieves its highest realization when it allows itself to be moved by God to live the supernatural virtue of charity. Augustine recognized that human freedom has limits, because we human beings are conditioned by our experiences, the culture in which we live, and our past decisions. Precisely because of these limits, the bishop of Hippo discerned that grace responds to the deepest desires of human freedom by opening up a transcendent horizon. As the theologian Eugene TeSelle comments, grace "invites or draws the affections, not overcoming free choice," enabling the soul "to be free for the first time."

The Church's Teaching on the Need for Grace

The North African bishops, firmly opposed to the errors spread by Pelagius, refuted his teaching in various councils. The condemnations from the Fifteenth Council of Carthage, which took place in the year 418, were confirmed by Pope Zosimus.

Zosimus had at first been reluctant to take such a step. The pope made the condemnation only after Emperor Honorius had issued an edict against Pelagius and Celestius for the riots and disorder caused by their movement. Pelagianism, indeed, tended to divide Christians between the holy and the damned, with no place for the middle ground of sinners. Because of Pelagius' great confidence in the power of human freedom, those who sinned were thought to be always willingly rejecting God.

By its approval of the Fifteenth Council of Carthage's teaching, the Church authoritatively accepted the teaching of Augustine on original sin and grace. The Council's first canon, or statement, against the teachings of Pelagius and Celestius states that death is not natural to Adam but rather is a consequence of sin. This truth has important ramifications for understanding human nature. In keeping with the testimony of Scripture (Gn 3:19; Rom 5:12), death is part of a broader perspective in which man's creaturely condition exists in a wounded and diminished state due to the sin of Adam.

The next canon, a consequence of the first, defends the Church's practice of baptizing infants for the remission of sins. The issue at hand was not simply the fact of infant baptism. As we have seen, the Pelagian position did not reject infant baptism. For Pelagius, baptism was necessary to enter the kingdom of heaven, but not—however odd it might sound—for the forgiveness of sins or to obtain eternal life.

In affirming the practice of infant baptism for remission of sins, the Council makes a strong declaration of just how much human nature is in need of God's grace. The Council bases its position on Paul's statement, in the Letter to the Romans, that "sin came into the world through one man and death through sin, and so death spread to all men because all men sinned" (Rom 5:12). Although infants have not personally committed sins, as the Council notes, they share in the state of sin because they are descendants of Adam.

The truth of the sinfulness of infants can be difficult to understand. Nonetheless, Augustine came to this conclusion not simply from the testimony of Scripture but also from his own observation of the way human beings are born into a world of suffering, marked by ignorance and selfishness. All these negative realities, the bishop of Hippo concluded, only make sense if all human beings in some way share in the guilt of Adam. Furthermore, we should also keep in mind that Augustine's stark analysis of human nature is above all meant to highlight the power of the liberation which is given to man through grace.

The next three canons of the Council of Carthage describe the way grace works in man. The Council places emphasis on our continual need for grace in action. In doing this, the assembly refuted a core assertion of Pelagius' teaching, which is that the human will has complete freedom to do good or evil. Pelagius, as noted previously, rejected the idea that our free will needs any help from outside of human nature. To the contrary, the third canon states that the grace of God not only brings about the forgiveness of sins, but moreover gives assistance so that we might not sin anymore. The implication here is that, even after the gift of grace, we still retain our sinful inclinations and remain continually in need of actual grace.

The Council went on to state that the grace of Christ not only gives us knowledge of the good but also "inspires us with a desire that we may be able to accomplish what we know." Here, the bishops of North Africa clarify the truth of grace against Pelagius' position that grace could work interiorly, but only to illuminate the mind. The Council, by contrast, teaches that grace gives us both knowledge and the charity to make this knowledge an effective reality.

The subsequent canon condemns the final aspect of Pelagius' view of human action. After acknowledging the ability to do the good, which comes from God, and the will to do good, which according to Pelagius would come only from man, Pelagius spoke of our innate capacity to *carry out* the good. In light of this view, the Council Fathers at Carthage state plainly that "without the grace of God we can do no good thing." Grace does not simply facilitate the good; it is necessary for the performance of the good, in light of the words of Christ: "Apart from me you can do nothing" (Jn 15:5).

Through this doctrine proclaimed at Carthage, the Church clearly articulated the reality of our sinful condition. She further described the way grace restores human nature and constantly is at work so that we might both will and actually carry out the good. The Council of Trent would return to this teaching in its decree on justification, when it described in detail the role of grace at every step in the Christian's journey toward God: from the beginnings of conversion, to the carrying out of good works, to the gift of final perseverance.

The Church, in fact, has continually felt the need to return to the truths which emerged from the Pelagian controversy. While Christians have a unique insight into the dignity of the human person and the reality of human freedom, we easily run the risk of losing sight of the extent to which grace must inspire and move our human efforts. Our tendency toward this narrowed vision of human action is itself a sign of our need for grace, but it also reflects the manner by which God's gift acts in the soul. Grace acts in a hidden and silent way in the depth of our being, like the "still small voice" in which God revealed himself to the prophet Elijah (1 Kgs 19:12).

Hence, as John Paul II pointed out at the beginning of the third millennium, we are constantly beset by the temptation of "thinking that the results depend on our ability to act and to plan." As a consequence, we need to continually return to the truths established by the Church's confrontation with Pelagianism. God, as the Polish pope noted, really asks us to cooperate with grace and place our efforts at his service. But this human element should never cause us to lose sight of that other reality which John Paul II wanted to once more remind the Church of: "It is fatal to forget that 'without Christ we can do nothing' (see Jn 15:5)."

CHAPTER 8

God's Grace and the Reality of Human Freedom

THE SPREAD OF PELAGIUS' TEACHING, as we saw in the last chapter, provided an opportunity for the Church to decisively affirm our need for grace. We have also noted that this necessity for grace, as well as the action of grace, coexists with the reality of human freedom.

These aspects of Christian action—freedom and grace—are not always easy to put together. Sometimes, in appreciating the action of God's grace, we might run the risk of not fully grasping that we remain free. Indeed, before the action of God it is not at all easy to comprehend how we can remain free. But we are indeed free before God, and our free response to God gives rise to the *good works* which are essential fruits of the Christian life. In this chapter, we will examine the mystery of man's free response to grace, as well as some more misunderstandings of this topic that have emerged over the centuries.

Man's Freedom before the Reality of Sin

Thomas Aquinas, taking up the doctrine of Augustine, recognized the way in which original sin introduced a disorder in man's powers. Our reason is no longer subject to God, our senses are no longer subordinate to reason, and the body is no longer at the service of the soul. As we have noted, the Christian tradition has come to use the word *concupiscence* to describe the way our desires, wounded by original sin, move against the dictates of reason.

Still, Aquinas is also cognizant that man, even with the corruption caused by original sin, has not lost all of his capacity to do good. Man in this state is not capable of doing supernatural good, yet he is capable of doing good at the natural level. The Angelic Doctor gives examples such as building homes and planting vineyards. However, as Aquinas also notes, just as a sick man might not be able to fully move and could need medical help, man in the state of sin is not fully able to carry out the good; he needs the help of grace to strengthen his nature and make it capable of supernatural good.

As we saw in chapter two, the Council of Trent affirmed the reality of our freedom in light of the teaching of Martin Luther. While Luther felt that concupiscence so dominated us to the extent that all our works are evil and sinful, the Council stated that we retain freedom in the face of our sinful inclinations. In fact, in the case of the baptized, the Council taught that concupiscence "cannot harm those who do not give consent but, by the grace of Christ, offer strong resistance." The Council's teaching reminds us that we can resist sin by grace, but also that such resistance depends on our own "consent." During the period after the Council of Trent, theologians became interested in the question of how freedom operates in relation to grace.

Scripture gives testimony to the reality that the person has the capacity to reject God. For example, Christ, in the Last Supper, speaks about the reality of a culpable repudiation of his preaching: "If I had not come and spoken to them, they would not have sin; but now they have no excuse for their sin" (Jn 15:22). In light of this truth, theologians have come to use the term *sufficient grace*. This grace enables the person to carry out a good act, but the will remains free to accept or refuse this influence. When the will consents, *efficacious grace* brings about the good action.

The concept of efficacious grace has a foundation in scriptural testimony about the power of God's grace. Grace is an action of God in the person, and at times revelation places emphasis on the way this action of God overcomes all resistance. We have made reference to God's promise, in the Book of Ezekiel, to put his spirit within his people, by which God would "cause" his people to walk according to his statutes (36:27). Christ gives witness to this power of God's will: "All that the Father gives me will come to me" (Jn 6:37).

The concept of *efficacious* grace points to an important aspect of grace, which exists alongside the reality of human freedom. This concept expresses the truth that God's grace has the power to overcome our resistance to grace and attachment to sin. This dimension of grace is manifested in Augustine's description of grace as *delectatio victrix* or "victorious pleasure." This description reflects the experience of Augustine's own conversion, and that of countless others who, in the course of their conversions, perceive the way grace seems to "take control" of the will. The bishop of Hippo's recognition of grace's potency led him to also speak of "invincible grace" (*gratia invicta*).

The terminology of sufficient and efficacious grace has its limits. We need to keep in mind that grace is not a "thing" that God sends us but rather a saving action of God. From this point of view, we can say that grace is always efficacious. If the creature resists, God will not perform his saving action, and we can say—as Juan Luis Lorda asserts—that there is no grace. Still, this terminology is a way of helping us to understand the reality of our freedom while at the same time acknowledging the efficacy or power of grace.

Despite the Council of Trent's dogmatic statements about the action of grace and the reality of freedom, there would continue to be misconceptions regarding these topics.

The Thought of Baius and Jansen Regarding Freedom and Grace

The issues brought up by Martin Luther led a number of Catholic theologians to examine the relationship of grace and freedom in light of Augustine's teaching. The sixteenth-century Belgian theologian Michel Baius sought to establish dialogue with Protestants and was among those who attempted to go back to the original teaching of the bishop of Hippo.

Baius recognized, like Augustine, the power of grace which acts by pouring out charity in the heart of the believer. However, in this later theologian's perspective, this action of grace takes place in a perspective in which man is completely corrupted by sin. For Baius, the reality of sin applies to fallen man regardless of whether there is a will to disobey God. Man, according to this view, has completely lost any freedom of choice due to original sin. Man is thus necessarily in a state of mortal sin and deserving of eternal punishment.

Baius' teaching bears a resemblance to certain points of Augustine's teaching regarding the reality of original sin and our need for grace. However, the Belgian theologian took this teaching out of context and in doing so produced a one-sided notion of grace, which left no room for human freedom. For Baius, we lack freedom even after receiving the gift of redemption. God's saving action, for him, would simply be a passing impulse, a "motion of the soul," by which God leads the soul to exercise supernatural charity. In this view, the action of grace does not bring about any transformation or *state* of grace within the soul.

Baius' position shows how an overemphasis on our sinful condition can also lead to a diminished appreciation of the meaning of grace. While Baius held that man's nature after original sin is profoundly marked by sin, the state of man before original sin would be one in which grace was unnecessary. In this latter state man, by his own merits, would have been able to gain access to the immediate vision of God. The grace brought by Christ, according to Baius, is not something beyond man's nature. Rather, what he calls *grace* would be the communion with God that God gave to man, as part of his nature, before original sin.

So, for this interpreter of Augustine, grace would not be a free gift of God that helps us to achieve an end—union with God—that goes beyond our nature. In this way, his position loses sight of the way God's grace is a free and unmerited gift, which opens us up to a new, supernatural dimension.

Hence Baius, while intending to go back to Scripture and the Fathers of the Church, ended up losing sight of the profound mystery presented by revelation. His position demonstrates the danger of emphasizing certain aspects of Scripture, such as the power of God's love and the reality of human sin, while at the same time ignoring other aspects. Additionally, Baius' interpretation of Augustine allows us to see how even such a great teacher as Augustine needs to be understood within his own context and also from a broader perspective. In this regard, we can note how the great doctors of the medieval period, and in particular Thomas Aquinas, stood out for their ability to approach the mystery of revealed truth in a penetrating and balanced manner.

Baius' teachings were thoroughly studied and then condemned by Pope St. Pius V in 1567, and later again by Pope Gregory XIII in 1579. The positions of the Belgian theologian are not compatible with Catholic teaching regarding the reality of man's freedom, and also conflict with the truth that grace is a gift that goes beyond man's nature.

Baius submitted to these condemnations and died in union with Church. Unfortunately, however, Baius' work and ideas would later spread widely through the *Jansenist* movement. The seventeenth-century thinker Cornelius Jansen, like Baius, was a professor of theology at the University of Louvain in Belgium. The atmosphere of the university in Jansen's time was still strongly influenced by the thought of Baius, and Jansen dedicated himself to the study of Augustine's thought on grace.

Jansen recognized the controversy that his ideas would bring about and was prudent in his teaching as a professor and later as a bishop. His important work, which Jansen entitled *Augustinus* out of his desire to be faithful to the great teacher on grace, would only be published after his death.

Jansenism was a reaction against a number of theologians, most notably the sixteenth-century Spanish Jesuit Luis de Molina, who affirmed the possibility of our cooperation with grace and the truth of our freedom. We will discuss Molina's thought later in this chapter. In the face of the theologians who emphasized human freedom, Jansen desired once more to return to certain aspects of what he thought to be Augustine's teaching.

Like Baius, Jansen emphasized the fallenness of the human condition after original sin, to the point that we lack all capacity to resist sin. Fallen man would therefore need the special grace of God, the "victorious pleasure" (*delectatio victrix*) of which Augustine spoke, in order to do good. Jansen understood this action of God in such a way that he left no room for human freedom. The attraction of grace would take power over the will, in such a manner that man would have no power to defy it. On the other hand, those who did not receive this grace would simply not be predestined for salvation.

Despite various condemnations by the Church, Jansen's ideas spread widely in Europe, especially in France, and continued to exert influence over the course of the following centuries. The French Abbey of Port-Royal served as a center for Jansenism and attracted influential members of society. The adherents of this movement were unsatisfied with the existing state of the Church, and so sought to return to what they saw as the "pure" Church of primitive times. Central to such a renewal, according to them, would be a return to the supposedly authentic teaching of Augustine.

Jansenism's awareness of the deeply depraved state of man, after original sin, paradoxically led to the demand for a high level of moral behavior. Because of our sinful state, Jansenists tended to think that there would be very few who reach salvation. Those who did make it to heaven would do so by a very special grace of God, which would lead them to live a heroic level of holiness. On the other hand, the great majority of people would be hopelessly marred by selfishness and worldliness. As a result, people were encouraged to stay away from Communion if they had the slightest doubt about their worthiness to receive this sacrament.

Many Jansenists were no doubt moved by authentic desires for spiritual renewal in the face of the worldliness and moral laxity present in society. Still, these desires led them to be overly negative in their attitude to the world and also toward authority in the Church. As in the case of Baius, the Jansenist movement serves as a reminder of the practical dangers that can arise from an unbalanced understanding of the mysteries of grace and human nature. Appreciating these mysteries and living according to them requires more than simply adherence to a set of writings, even those of a teacher as important as Augustine. Rather, we can see nature and grace in their true dimensions only through a humble adherence to the mystery revealed by God, a mystery that is faithfully and dynamically passed on by the Church through her teaching office.

The *de Auxiliis* Controversy

The ideas of Baius and later Jansen, as we have noted, were connected to another important debate regarding the relationship between grace and freedom. A key moment in this other debate was the publication of the work *On the Harmony of Free Will with the Gifts of Grace, Divine Foreknowledge, Predestination and Reprobation* by Luis de Molina in the year 1588. In the face of the theological visions that downplayed the reality of man's freedom, both among Protestants and Catholics, Molina desired to defend the reality of man's free will.

Molina held that the human will, even when under the action of grace, always retains the freedom to reject grace. According to his view, God gives sufficient grace to all; this grace becomes efficacious grace when the person freely accepts it.

The avowal of this freedom led to a theological problem. How do we reconcile our freedom with the reality of God's authority over history and creation? Thomas Aquinas had taught that God is the first cause of all things, and that God guides creation in accord with divine providence. The reality that God is the *primary* cause behind the world, as Aquinas notes, does not take away from the fact that there can be *secondary* causes. God has willed that some of these secondary causes, such as human beings, possess freedom.

While Aquinas' perspective helps us to comprehend how God's all-powerful will can exist alongside the reality of human freedom, we might still ask: If God guides all things to his loving end, how does he take account of our freedom? For Aquinas, God already knows all of humanity's future actions, including those that depend on human freedom. Molina felt that, in order to safeguard the reality of freedom, it was necessary to propose that God has a "middle knowledge" (*scientia media*). This middle knowledge would include those things which depend on the free will of creatures.

With this *scientia media*, God contemplates all the possible ways in which persons could freely respond to his grace, in all possible circumstances. Out of all these possibilities, God brings about the world that he chooses. God also gives us the gift of grace based on his knowledge of how we will freely respond to it. In this way, God remains free in his divine action of creating and giving the gift of grace, but we also remain free to accept or reject grace.

Molina's novel views about freedom were sharply contested, in particular by the Spanish Dominican Domingo Báñez. Báñez saw Molina's position as a rejection of the traditional teaching regarding the efficacy of God's grace, a teaching rooted in Augustine and Aquinas.

Báñez approached the mysteries of grace and freedom from a different angle than Molina. While Molina used the reality of human freedom as his starting point, Báñez parted from the awareness that God is the first cause behind all of creation. For the Dominican theologian, God is able to determine man's free will toward a particular way of acting. In this view, God's grace would have an infallible strength to lead man's will according to God's desire. For Báñez, this predetermining action of God would not take away human freedom, because God would be moving the human will in such a way that this will would act in harmony with man's own nature, without any coercion from the outside.

The disputes regarding Molina's and Báñez's positions became so intense that in 1597, Pope Clement VIII decided to set up a commission in Rome to study each school of thought. Most of the members of the commission felt that Molina's teaching was contrary to the teaching of Augustine and Thomas Aquinas. However, many defended Molina and saw problems with Báñez's teaching on the way God predetermines the human will. After eighty-five sessions and forty-seven debates, the pope—by that time Paul V—declared that each of the positions could be taught and prohibited theologians on either side from refuting the other side's conviction.

Looking back at the controversy four centuries later, we can better see the way the positions of Molina and Báñez capture different aspects of the mysterious interaction between our free will and God's grace. Molina's view helps us to perceive the need to adequately account for the freedom we have before grace. At the same time, Báñez's theory points to another significant reality, which is that God's grace mysteriously acts within our will, moving it toward God and leading it to experience the fullness of freedom. This full realization of our freedom comes precisely when God's grace takes hold of the will and fills it with his love.

This union between the reality of freedom and the power of grace has particular relevance in our society today. Too often, we place great emphasis on our own individual freedom but without giving adequate attention to God's action. The Church's reflection on these mysteries over the centuries helps us to understand how freedom and grace are distinct realities, and yet not opposed to one another. As St. Josemaría Escrivá states, "Freedom finds its true meaning when it is put to the service of the truth which redeems, when it is spent in seeking God's infinite Love which liberates us from all forms of slavery."

Grace, Good Works, and Merit

We can grasp the full reality of human freedom, as it cooperates with grace, in the good works which are a hallmark of the Christian life. Christ calls his followers to let their "light so shine before men, that they may see your good works and give glory to your Father who is in heaven" (Mt 5:16). In keeping with this truth, the Christian tradition speaks of the possibility of gaining *merit* before God.

In view of the truths that we have studied up to now, perhaps the notions of "good works" and "merit" can make us feel uneasy. The human being is in need of God's grace to be able to carry out any genuinely good action. As a consequence, we might feel that the concepts of "good works" and "merit" prevent us from adequately valuing the essential role of grace.

However, we have also seen that a defining characteristic of grace is that it refers to an action of God *in us*. If grace were simply about God, we would not need to use the term *grace*. But in fact, grace refers to the profound reality by which God raises up and elevates our own nature to a new supernatural level of being. From this point of view, we can better comprehend how grace, far from taking away what is proper to human nature, gives the human being a new capacity of being and acting.

Hence, the power of grace is shown particularly in that it becomes present in our action and in our works. This is an important truth to remember today, as many people think that the presence of grace somehow dispenses us from the need to actually live a moral life in keeping with the commandments. In contrast to such ideas, John Paul II wanted to emphasize—the italics are his—that the gift of grace "*does not lessen but reinforces the moral demands of love*." Grace in fact allows the person to live the commandments in their fullest sense, by practicing Christ's new commandment of love (Jn 13:34–35).

In light of these demands of the Christian moral life, Catholic theology has developed the notion of *merit*. While this concept was only developed during the Middle Ages, it reflects the notion of *reward* which appears frequently in both the Old and New Testaments. In the Old Testament, God frequently promises material prosperity to his people for their obedience to him; we can think for example of the "land which flows with milk and honey" that God promises (Nm 14:8). Christ often speaks about reward, both directly and through parables. Even the one who gives a cup of cold water to a disciple "shall not lose his reward" (Mt 10:42).

Considering these and other texts of Scripture, we can speak about the merit that we can obtain before God. We cannot carry out the good in the deepest sense without God's grace, and so we cannot really merit anything on our own. Strictly speaking, God is infinitely above us, and we do not have the "right" to anything before God.

However, the reality of grace radically changes this situation. Through grace, God has freely elevated us so as to share in his own life. As a result, through this sharing in the divine life, we can say that we have a certain "right" to eternal life. In this state man, as Aquinas points out, "is adopted as a son of God, to whom the inheritance is due by right of adoption, according to Romans 8:17: 'If sons, heirs also.'"

In view of the promises which God has freely made to man, theologians in the Middle Ages came to use the term *condign* merit. This refers to the reward due for our good actions; not for the value of these actions *per se*, but because God has committed himself to granting this reward. God has decreed that, through Christ and the gift of the Holy Spirit, our response to God might give us a certain right to eternal life, and also—as the Council of Trent teaches—a right to an increase in grace.

In addition, theologians speak of *congruent* merit, which refers to a reward given not because of a "right" but because of the goodness of God. We can see this form of merit as a consequence of the Christian's identity as a son or daughter of God. In addition to the promise of eternal life, Christ has promised that the Father will grant to Christ's followers other "good things": "If you then, who are evil, know how to give good gifts to your children, how much more will your Father who is in heaven give good things to those who ask him!" (Mt 7:11). In keeping with this awareness of our state of friendship with God through grace, the Church teaches that we can merit graces for ourselves and for others, and even merit temporal goods such as health and friendship.

As we noted in chapter five, Martin Luther placed great emphasis on how justification is a free and gratuitous act of God. In line with this vision, Luther rejected the idea that we have "rights" before God, and he, and Protestants in general, have denied the possibility of merit on the part of man. Luther certainly had a valid point, and in light of this, the Church has been careful to clarify that merit does not belong to us, except by God's freely given grace.

Still, the authentic meaning of merit is thoroughly in harmony with the reality of justification in man. Augustine himself, who so deeply emphasized man's fallenness and the need for grace, also realized that justified man can win merit for eternal life. In granting us the possibility of merit, Augustine comments, God does not so much crown our merits, but rather he crowns God's own gift.

This teaching of Augustine had great importance during the Middle Ages, and the Council of Trent desired to recall it when the Council clarified the authentic nature of Christian merit. The Council declares that justification is the fruit of the merit of Christ and specifically of Christ's passion. The strength of Christ Jesus himself, the Council's decree on justification affirms, continually grants strength to the justified. This strength, as the decree notes, "always precedes, accompanies and follows their good works, and without it they would be wholly unable to do anything meritorious and pleasing to God." The merit of Christ is the font through which the Christian performs good works and thus, as the decree also notes, merits an increase of grace, eternal life, and also an increase of glory in heaven.

In approaching the mysteries of grace and freedom, God's initiative and our voluntary cooperation, faith and good works, we therefore need to avoid creating undue oppositions. As the *Catechism* points out, "The grace of Christ is not in the slightest way a rival of our freedom when this freedom accords with the sense of the true and the good that God has put in the human heart." God offers us the free gift of his grace previous to any response on our part. At the same time, this grace seeks to stimulate our free response and gives full meaning to freedom. As the twentieth-century German theologian Johann Auer observes, God and man are both totally involved in each salvific action.

So, far from opposing grace and freedom to one another, the Christian faith leads us to see how these elements work in harmony. As the *Catechism* also teaches, the more we respond to the action of grace, the more we grow in true interior freedom: "By the working of grace the Holy Spirit educates us in spiritual freedom in order to make us free collaborators in his work in the Church and in the world." Hence, our study of grace and freedom should lead us to a heightened awareness of the value of Christian *works*, the fruit of grace. The grace of God calls the believer to an intense life of prayer, sacrifice, and action, so that the Christian might merit to receive, from the fullness of merits of Christ, "grace upon grace" (Jn 1:16).

CHAPTER 9

Grace, Freedom, and God's Plan of Salvation

THE TRUTHS REGARDING GRACE that we have examined up to now could lead to still more questions. For example, we might ask: How exactly does grace act in us? How is it that grace seems to work in some but not in others? Does God have favorites?

Theologians have grappled with these questions for centuries. As we have seen, justification and sanctification are gratuitous actions in which God takes the initiative. As Christ says, "The Son gives life to whom he will" (Jn 5:21). The workings of grace, in the final analysis, will go beyond our understanding. What Christ says with regard to the Holy Spirit also applies to the mysterious action of God within man: "You do not know whence it comes or whither it goes" (Jn 3:8).

In this chapter we want to delve more deeply into the way grace acts in us. The Church's reflection on this topic has sought to uphold the reality of human freedom while at the same time offering insight into the saving plan of God that comes before and guides this freedom.

The Semi-Pelagian Controversy: The Debate on the Beginning of Faith and Predestination

In chapter eight, we studied how the Church embraced the teachings of Augustine with regard to our need for grace. This step did not bring an end to controversy.

Indeed, in the intense atmosphere of his debate with Pelagianism, Augustine made some strong statements to emphasize the gratuity of God's grace. The bishop of Hippo wanted to highlight how God's gift of grace is totally independent of any effort on our part. In making this argument, Augustine stated that God had created human nature as good, but due to Adam's sin, all of human nature has participated in sin and would be deserving of damnation. Only the grace of God, he held, can save fallen man from condemnation.

These ideas caused consternation among the monks of the north African city Hadrumetum. These monks were concerned about the implications of Augustine's teaching for monastic life. The bishop of Hippo's teaching could lead one to ask: If the grace of God is the central factor behind salvation, what would be the point of the energetic exhortations to live out the virtues which are so central to the ascetical life? In fact, some of the monks were arguing that, if their will was really dependent upon God, their abbot should stop correcting them.

In the face of this agitation, the abbot of the monastery at Hadrumetum wrote to Augustine. He asked if, in light of the bishop of Hippo's teaching on grace, it would be purposeless to make corrections or admonitions aimed at helping others to live virtue.

In response to these concerns, Augustine wrote two treatises dealing with the relationship between grace and free will. He insisted on the reality of our free will as a truth strongly attested to by Scripture. The Word of God encourages us to do good and avoid evil, he noted, and such indications would make no sense if we did not have free will.

However, Augustine went on to emphasize that, without the assistance of grace, our free will would be incapable of fulfilling the law. The will, according to this doctor of the church, needs to be converted, so that it might both desire to fulfill God's law and carry out the law. On the other hand, in certain cases Scripture tells us that God hardens the heart of persons who are bent on committing evil, as in the case of Pharoah at the time of Israel's slavery (Ex 7:3). In these cases, Augustine says that God has allowed the human will to turn to evil, although the evil remains an action carried out by human agency.

In the course of Augustine's work, the notion of *predestination* took on great importance. According to this notion, as the bishop of Hippo understood it, justification is based purely on a free choice on God's part, with no merit at all on our part. Augustine pointed to the words of the apostle Paul, among other Scripture texts: "For those whom he foreknew he also predestined to be conformed to the image of his Son" (Rom 8:29).

Here, Augustine took a step further from his earlier position, discussed in chapter seven, that the human being would be capable of desiring the good without grace. In the face of this discrepancy, he would only offer the explanation that, after having written in favor of human free will, "God's grace conquered."

The questions posed to Augustine and Augustine's response would give rise to a new debate, which has come to be known as the "Semi-Pelagian" controversy, even though it is distinct from the Pelagian episode. In this polemic, Augustine would accentuate ever more deeply the degree to which grace is absolutely necessary for the human will. His intention, as we have mentioned, was to stress even more the gratuity of grace. Even in the case of rewards for good works, the bishop of Hippo notes, God is rewarding grace for the works which are themselves a grace.

Augustine certainly did not want to eliminate the reality of our freedom or denigrate the effort and struggle of Christians to live the virtues. He was, however, trying to put the exercise of freedom within a bigger picture, in which God's grace is the essential element for us to act well.

Despite Augustine's attempts at clarification, the resistance to his teaching spread, especially in southern Gaul (present-day France), which had become a site of vibrant monasticism. Many monks there felt that Augustine's teaching on the priority of God's will contradicted the reality of human freedom. They asserted that there must be some beginning in the human will by which the person might obtain or receive grace.

In response to these critiques, Augustine wrote the final two works of his life: *On the Predestination of the Saints* and *On the Gift of Perseverance*. In the first treatise, Augustine desired to revise his earlier work in such a way that there would be absolutely no human element that came before grace. Previously, he had held that justification might be based on God's foreknowledge of whether a person would respond by faith. As he meditated more deeply on the mystery of Scripture, Augustine came to the conviction that justification must always be attributed to a free choice on God's part. Among other texts, he cites Paul's letter to the Romans: "At the present time there is a remnant, chosen by grace" (Rom 11:5).

In his treatise on perseverance, the bishop of Hippo drew out the conclusion of the principle he had established in his work on predestination. God is at the very beginning of the work of justification, and God is also the one who brings about the end of the work of grace, that is, final perseverance in the Christian life. Perseverance is a gift, Augustine states, since God commands that we pray "Lead us not into temptation" in the Lord's Prayer.

From his own life as well as from his own pastoral experience, the north African bishop and theologian realized how even those persons who are deeply committed Christians, perhaps for many years, always retain the possibility of turning their backs on God. As Peter Brown points out, this stark reality of human weakness led Augustine to seek a more stable foundation in God's decision, and specifically in the notion of predestination. Why are some faithful to God while others are not? For Augustine, the answer to this question can only be found in the free choice of God.

The bishop of Hippo describes perseverance as a gift of God that cannot be taken away. If God grants this gift, we will certainly persevere; if the gift is not bestowed, we will not persevere until the end. In the latter case, the fault would lie with the person who has forsaken God by his own will.

These explanations did not satisfy Augustine's critics. They felt that Augustine was lessening the value of human freedom and proclaiming a God who unjustly condemns. However, we should keep in mind that Augustine himself knew that he could not make the mysteries of faith completely intelligible. Before the question of why God would show his mercy to some and not to others, the bishop of Hippo can only respond: "I confess that I can find no answer to make." While recognizing the righteousness of God's anger and the greatness of his mercy, Augustine acknowledges that God's "judgments are unsearchable."

This sense of humility before the mystery of God's revelation is a key characteristic of Augustine's thought on grace. At the most fundamental level, predestination is a truth manifested by God, while freedom and the need for human effort are also revealed truths. Augustine does not desire to say that persons should not respond to God's grace with their own effort. Rather, the man known as the "Doctor of Grace" wanted Christians to understand that when they respond to God's grace, God is the one who always comes first. He is the one who has known them and chosen them in advance, precisely so that they might correspond freely to his love. Augustine comments that the awareness of this truth helps the Christian to glory "not in himself, but in the Lord."

In subsequent decades, proponents of both positions—those who emphasized with Augustine the priority of divine grace, and those who tried to give more weight to the human will—engaged in fierce debate. The opponents of Augustine caricatured the bishop of Hippo's position, while Augustine's defenders ended up adjusting their great doctor's own positions.

Looking back, centuries later, we can appreciate how each side was looking at the mystery of grace from a different angle. Augustine and his followers focused on the mystery of God's design as revealed in Scripture, while the monks in southern Gaul were concerned with the need for a moral struggle to live an upright life. This latter concern led St. John Cassian, the head of a community of monks in southern Gaul during the fifth century, to assert that *both* grace and free will are needed for a salvific act. Another fifth-century monk from the same area who became a bishop, Faustus of Riez, later took a similar position. After Augustine's death in the year 430, his fifth-century lay disciple St. Prosper of Aquitaine and the sixth-century archbishop St. Caesarius of Arles (AD 502–542), both also from the present-day south of France, would champion the teaching of Augustine.

The Second Council of Orange and the Resolution of the Semi-Pelagian Controversy

The opponents of Augustine's teaching on grace viewed the interaction of grace and human action from a different perspective from that of the bishop of Hippo. This vision had developed in the eastern part of the Church. This distinct conception, rooted in the thought of the third-century theologian Origen of Alexandria, had emphasized how self-initiated divine action and self-initiated human action would go together. Cassian recognized that in a monastic context it was essential to help the monks to be aware of their responsibility for their actions, and in this respect Augustine's ideas seemed to pose a threat.

It is also important to note that the Greek-speaking Fathers of the Church often used language that highlighted the need for the exercise of the will in the practice of the virtues, but without always making explicit mention of the need for grace. In this respect, we can say that Augustine helped draw attention to the deeper dynamic of grace that lies behind all of the believer's efforts to live virtue. But Augustine, as we have noted, did not want to do away with the need for ascetical struggle.

Caesarius was the right person to facilitate bringing an end to the Semi-Pelagian controversy. He was raised in the monastic environment of southern Gaul, in which the opposition to Augustine was strongly rooted, but also received extensive schooling in the thought of Augustine. He had a deeply pastoral sense which allowed him to bring together an awareness of the priority of grace with the need for repentance and good works. His theological views are largely contained in his sermons.

In keeping with the earlier monastic tradition, he often accentuated the need to carry out the good without always speaking about the need for grace. However, Caesarius' emphasis on the need for human action stemmed from a deep awareness of the transforming power of grace. The archbishop of Arles had a keen consciousness of the transformation that occurs in baptism, through which our freedom is restored and the Christian is empowered to choose the good. Caesarius' awareness of this new reality, brought about by grace, led him to a deep sense of the Christian's responsibility to use his freedom well.

The Church historian Rebecca Harden Weaver, in her extensive study of the Semi-Pelagian controversy, notes that Caesarius was Augustinian in thought but also made significant adjustments to the thought of the illustrious bishop of Hippo. Because Caesarius saw the Christian life as a continuous struggle whose outcome could not be known until death, Caesarius changed Augustine's teachings about perseverance and predestination. For the archbishop of Arles, perseverance was not simply the result of a divine decree but would depend on the Christian's own free action to hold fast to the good.

Caesarius' theological view on perseverance therefore appears to differ from that of Augustine. For the Doctor of Grace, God's gift of perseverance always acts infallibly, and God's predestination is the sole cause of salvation. Caesarius recognized the New Testament teaching regarding a predestination to grace. He asserted, like Augustine, that man is in need of *prevenient* grace, that is, a grace that comes before any action of the will. Such grace would be a necessary condition for the human will to be restored to grace and directed to God. Nonetheless, for this Gallic archbishop, God's predestination is not the all-determining factor as in Augustine.

In the year 529, Caesarius presided over the Second Council of Orange, once again in what is now southern France. The assembly was aimed at resolving the Semi-Pelagian controversy. The propositions approved by the Council, and later by the pope, were largely drawn from writings of Augustine and Prosper of Aquitaine.

The canons of the Council are a vigorous affirmation of the priority of grace over any human merit. They remind us that while grace and human response are both important, we can never see them as operating on the same level, or in any way equivalent to one another. The Council teaches that grace always comes *before* man.

Grace comes before any prayer to God, and in fact it is always grace which leads us to pray (canon 3). The very will to be cleansed from sin, the Council declares, comes from God (canon 4). The very beginning and desire for faith are also gifts of grace (canon 5). Furthermore, in carrying out any good act, we are in need of God's continual assistance (canon 6). The Council goes so far as to state that even God's love for us is not for who we are, but in light of the gift of grace that he desires to grant us (canon 12).

This deep need for grace is in part due to the fact that our freedom has been impaired due to sin. However, the Council also notes that even if human nature had not been damaged by sin, it would still need the grace of God for salvation (canon 19).

This absolute priority of grace does not blur the truth of our own capacity for action. The Second Council of Orange recognizes that our will has been purified by grace, and as a result we have the "ability and responsibility" to cooperate with grace in the process of salvation.

Significantly, the Council makes no endorsement of the idea that the just are infallibly predestined to glory through a special gift of God. In fact, the only specific mention of predestination is to reject the notion that persons are predestined to evil by God. Such teaching does not mean that the Council rejected the notion of predestination. In fact, as Harden Weaver points out, the idea that God gives prevenient grace suggests that God makes a choice ahead of time to give his grace. Still, the Council wanted to avoid an idea of predestination that would prescind from the exercise of human freedom.

Our survey of this historical controversy reveals that much of Augustine's teaching on grace would come to be taken up as the Church's doctrine. Nonetheless, the Church has not wanted to confirm all of Augustine's reflections on grace. The Semi-Pelagian episode would help to bring about a greater harmony between grace, the reality of man's freedom, and God's saving will.

Such a harmony is essential for the Church's life and teaching. Christians have a unique recognition of God's completely free love for them, which precedes any merit on their part. At the same time, this recognition of the priority of grace can never take away the need for human cooperation and struggle. Grace does not take away the Christian's struggle for virtue, but it gives this struggle a new vitality and direction.

Predestination and God's Will for All to Be Saved

We noted in chapter one that predestination is an important scriptural concept which expresses God's choice to raise us to communion with the divine life through Christ. In emphasizing this theme, Augustine wanted to stress the initiative and mercy of God in a culture in which virtue could often be seen as the result of human effort.

As the centuries went by, there was the danger of understanding this viewpoint of Augustine outside of its original context. The ninth-century theologian and monk Gottschalk of Orbais, who lived in present-day Germany and France, was influenced by the teaching of Augustine and taught the doctrine of *double predestination*. According to this notion, God predestined some to salvation and others to condemnation. Therefore, for Gottschalk, Christ died only for those predestined for salvation.

These positions were not part of the teaching of Augustine, although it is true that they bear a certain resemblance to his ideas. But for Augustine, as we have noted, the emphasis is on how God's action of predestination reflects God's desire to save us. In the bishop of Hippo's thought, there is no predestination to condemnation, although Augustine does recognize that we would be justly condemned if not for God's saving action.

The Second Council of Orange, as we have noted, refuted the notion that man can be predestined to evil. In response to Gottschalk's teaching, the Council of Quiercy affirmed that Christ died for all. This latter Council clarified, as Juan Luis Lorda notes, that there is no parallelism between predestination and condemnation. God's action of predestination is oriented to salvation; condemnation, on the other hand, is the result of man's own free will.

The Protestant reformers would put a renewed emphasis on the concept of double predestination, although the major reformers understood this idea in different ways. Double predestination fit into the theological atmosphere of the time, in which many placed great value on the absolute power of God at the expense of our free will. While Martin Luther's views regarding this subject changed during his lifetime, he eventually came to the conviction—which he thought to be rooted in the Bible and Augustine—that God wills some to salvation and others to condemnation. However, this view was not taken up as a Lutheran doctrine.

The Reform movement initiated by the sixteenth-century Frenchman John Calvin has held predestination to be a key principle. For Calvin, double predestination was a consequence of two of his other key convictions: the absolute sovereignty of God and our radical incapacity to contribute to salvation. Calvin affirmed that God's eternal decree is at the basis of each person's eternal destiny, whether to eternal life or to eternal damnation. Calvin himself was repulsed by the idea that God would predestine souls to condemnation, but he felt that this punishment was just and also a means for manifesting God's glory. For this reformer, the eternal decrees of God do not take away our freedom from external coercion. Rather, we fall into sin and condemnation if God refuses to bestow grace upon us.

Calvin was moved by a sincere desire to recognize the sovereignty of God's will over the human will. His thought reminds us that it is difficult to recognize God's power and transcendence over all creation, and at the same time admit the real power of human freedom. Nonetheless, the Council of Trent asserted that the realities of God's power and human response need to be maintained, however challenging they might be for us to understand. This council declared that the action of grace in the soul is due to a previous call on the part of God, who gives us a "predisposing grace" that precedes any merit on our part. At the same time, the assembly at Trent negated the idea that God would not grant grace to some people, as if they were predestined to evil. The Council also stressed that, even after receiving the grace of justification, we still retain the possibility of turning away from God.

The clarifications made at Trent helped to dispel an exaggerated notion of predestination, but they certainly did not eliminate the mystery contained in this biblical concept. The Northern Irish theologian Alister McGrath points out that at Trent it was easier to reject erroneous views than to provide an authoritative statement on the subject, since among Catholics there were various views. Indeed, one of the most important lessons from the controversies regarding predestination is that human reason will easily fail if it tries to penetrate this mystery too deeply. Predestination is a truth revealed by God which reminds us of God's inscrutable action, before which human reason will always fall short.

We can, however, say that predestination is always a predestination to salvation. As Paul states, God "desires all men to be saved and to come to the knowledge of the truth" (1 Tm 2:4). Over the centuries, the Church has arrived at an ever-greater awareness of the way this saving action of God works. The Church has perceived that she has been sent by God to bring the grace of Jesus Christ to humanity, especially through baptism and the other sacraments. At the same time, theologians have also appreciated that the desire for baptism, or at least an implicit desire for it, could be a means by which the grace of justification reaches man.

The European settlement of the Americas in the fifteenth and sixteenth centuries led theologians to reflect more deeply on the ways in which grace operates in those who have never had the opportunity to hear the gospel message. In more recent centuries, the Church has realized that persons can be *invincibly ignorant* of the truth of the faith, which means that they are unaware of the truth of Christ due to no moral fault on their part. In the world in which we live, perhaps it is not difficult to perceive how such ignorance can exist for a complex set of social, cultural, and psychological reasons.

Thomas Aquinas explains how God's grace can operate in such situations. He describes a *first moral option* which we have at the very moment we reach the age of reason. At that moment, if we direct ourselves to our final end, we can obtain—through the action of grace—the forgiveness of original sin. In the case of the *ordinary* path of salvation, this grace will involve baptism in water and visible incorporation into the Church.

However, in cases where awareness of Christ and the Church is not present, God's grace can reach the soul through an *extraordinary* path. For such persons, as John Paul II comments, salvation can be obtained through a grace which, "while having a mysterious relationship to the Church, does not make them formally part of the Church but enlightens them in a way which is accommodated to their spiritual and material situation."

In both paths, the grace that unites us to God comes from Christ through the action of the Holy Spirit. This grace also unites us to the Church, which is made up of all those who have also reached union with God. Grace always comes from the Church, which is the means by which Christ communicates "truth and grace to all." Furthermore, grace always leads to unity with the Church, even if in the extraordinary cases this unity is not a visible one.

The Church's consciousness of the activity of grace, outside of her own visible dimension, in no way diminishes the need to evangelize. In fact, as the Church stated during the Jubilee Year 2000, the new People of God in Christ must go out to meet the desires of those in whom the Holy Spirit is at work, often in hidden ways. The Church, moved by charity and with the greatest respect for freedom, must proclaim "the truth definitively revealed by the Lord" and announce "the necessity of conversion to Jesus Christ and of adherence to the Church through Baptism and the other sacraments, in order to participate fully in communion with God, the Father, Son and Holy Spirit."

The Church carries out this mission with the awareness of God's loving plan of salvation, by which grace is mysteriously at work in human hearts, preceding and inspiring human actions, and leading men and women to an ever-deeper participation in the divine life.

CHAPTER 10

The Progress and Final End of the Life of Grace

OVER THE COURSE OF THIS WORK, we have sought to analyze how grace works in us. We have looked at how Catholic theology articulates the manner in which grace elevates the soul and mobilizes our freedom to its fullest realization. In the process, we have been reflecting on truths which have been revealed by God. However, as we know, these truths are never simply abstract ideas. They are truths that should be a living reality in the words and deeds of Christians.

In this chapter, we will study more specifically how grace operates in the day-to-day life of a Christian. This perspective is proper to *spiritual theology*, which is that branch of theology which tries to understand the unfolding of the spiritual life in the Christian. Many of these ideas may be familiar to us from our knowledge and practice of our faith. In any case, considering the spiritual life in relation to the truths about grace can offer us new lights to understand and live our vocation as sons of God in Christ.

The Baptismal Gift of Divine Filiation and Its Meaning

The transforming action of grace, received in particular through the sacrament of baptism, should have a profound impact in the Christian's daily life. Christianity uniquely recognizes a God whom we do not simply adore as God, but a God who has entered radically into the believer's life. As the Spanish theologian José Luis Illanes points out, the love which unites the Father, the Son, and the Holy Spirit with one another has been poured out upon us. By the action of the Holy Spirit which incorporates us into Christ, the Christian can live out an intimate and personal relationship with each one of these three divine Persons.

Through this action of God, the believer's entire life can exist in *relation* to the Trinity, and through this union with God his life becomes constituted in relation to others. This reality opens up a completely new perspective regarding the practice of virtue. The pre-Christian notion of virtue focused on the individual and put emphasis on self-perfection and self-dominion. The Christian, by contrast, is called to live his life in ever-greater relation with God and others.

The myriad forms of Christian prayer—which include vocal, liturgical, meditative, and contemplative prayer—are privileged means by which the Christian lives out the deep personal communion that flows from the action of grace. The great saints have described prayer as akin to the intimate and trusting relationship proper to persons in love. The sixteenth-century Carmelite St. Teresa of Ávila described contemplative prayer as "nothing else than an intimate sharing between friends."

Such images are an attempt to express, within the limits of language and human thought, a reality that goes above and beyond all human experience. We need to keep this in mind when we try to comprehend the spiritual life. In the deepest sense, God is not "like" a close friend. By means of grace, God is not simply close to us, but the Trinity dwells *within* us in our inmost being. The communion present within God's own

Trinitarian life, which contains relations of love far grander than any human love, is the model and source of the Christian life.

This truth has significant consequences. Many people today suffer from loneliness and a lack of stable relationships. Others are led to sadness because they put too much of their hopes in their relationship with another person, however worthy of love that person might be. In light of this reality, the Christian faith reminds us—as we noted in chapter one—that by our nature we are called to nothing less than personal union with God himself. Only in the communion with the Holy Trinity will man's hopes and desires be completely fulfilled, and only in this communion will other noble human relationships find their true dimension.

We have seen, in chapters three and four, how the Christian cries out to God with the cry *Abba* (Gal 4:6), an invocation used to indicate the close relationship that a small child has with his father. However, here again we need to purify these human images in light of the truths of faith. This is all the more important because human fathers, however admirable they may be, will inevitably have their limits. At times human fathers are absent or don't fulfill their duties.

Such human limitations do not affect in the least the truth of God's fatherhood. As we saw in chapter four, the fatherhood of God is the perfect image, source, and maximum realization of all fatherhood. Christ reveals the true nature of the Father, full of that tenderness and compassion which we see in the father of the Prodigal Son (Lk 15:22–24).

This special awareness of God's fatherhood has many concrete manifestations in the Christian's life. St. Josemaría Escrivá spoke about the "sense" of divine filiation which is a foundation for the Christian's spiritual life. By the word *sense*, the Spanish saint refers to something more than simply the knowledge that

God is a father, and more than even the intellectual awareness of this truth which comes through faith. This sense means that the person "feels" or experiences God's fatherhood in an immediate way, in his thoughts, desires, and affections.

The "sense" of divine filiation is a perceptible reminder that the new identity brought about by grace should also lead to a new way of thinking and acting on the part of the Christian. In the Sermon on the Mount, Christ describes a whole series of characteristics which distinguish the followers of Christ from others: faithfulness in marriage, the serenity that comes from trust in God's fatherly care, charity toward enemies, and the sincere prayer to the Father from the heart (Mt 5–6). In these and countless other ways the Christian gives testimony that the life of grace, while it remains hidden to human vision (Col 3:3), is a reality that has tangible and visible manifestations.

The revealed truth regarding grace, as we have seen, reminds us that our access to God the Father always takes place *through* Christ and always *in* the Holy Spirit. The Lord's Prayer only makes mention of the Father, but as the *Catechism of the Catholic Church* points out, this prayer to the Father takes place together with the Son and Holy Spirit.

This truth has decisive ramifications for how the Christian lives the reality of divine filiation. While the Christian can relate to God with the intimacy of a son with his father, this intimacy is never purely a "direct" access to the Father. It is always an access to the Father which takes place through Christ, the only begotten Son of God (Jn 14:6). This affirmation does not weaken the profound reality of God the Father's closeness, but it does remind us that this closeness always takes place in relation to Christ, and by means of the real and permanent identification with Christ that begins with baptism.

As noted in chapter four, the Christian is not "like Christ" or even "very close to Christ," but in light of baptism we can say that the Christian, in an imperfect yet real sense, *is* "Christ himself" or *ipse Christus*.

This mysterious reality does not do away with the Christian's own specific identity as a person, nor with the distance between creature and Creator. At the same time, the Christian's sacramental identification with Christ powerfully indicates the way grace brings about a new principle of being, and has manifold consequences for the spiritual life. Since the Christian always lives the reality of divine filiation in relation to Christ, he is always called to look to Christ as the model and source for growing in the sense of divine filiation.

Identification with Christ as Goal of the Spiritual Life

Building on the testimony of the New Testament, the liturgy and the Christian spiritual tradition have pointed to *identification with Christ* as a central goal in the spiritual life. Baptism marks the beginning of Christ's life in the Christian, and from this inception God desires this life to grow "to the measure of the stature of the fulness of Christ" (Eph 4:13). The believer lives as a son or daughter of God precisely by imitating the only begotten Son of God, who reveals to us the face of God in a fully human nature (Jn 14:9). As the Second Vatican Council comments, by his incarnation Christ is the perfect man, who "worked with human hands, . . . thought with a human mind, acted by human choice and loved with a human heart," and whom the Christian is called to imitate.

As the Spanish theologian Fernando Ocáriz has commented, this identification with Christ is never simply a question of imitating Christ as if he were an "external model." Such was the mistaken view of Pelagius, who failed to perceive the genuine reality of grace. Rather, the imitation of Christ is the unfolding of a reality which is already present in the Christian's soul, through the permanent identification with Christ that is received in baptism, strengthened by confirmation, and nourished in the Eucharist and in the other practices of the Christian life.

In analyzing this lived reality of the Christian's life, we can comprehend how the baptismal identification with Christ is at once a magnificent action of God and yet at the same time just a beginning. As Illanes points out, Christ is present in the Christian as a "dynamic principle" which is meant to reach fullness. Hence, the Christian is at once identified with Christ, but this very identification also leads him to live in an ever-deeper personal union of faith and love with Christ. The apostle Paul testifies to these two aspects when he comments that, on one hand, Christ has assumed dominance over Paul's own "I": "I have been crucified with Christ; it is no longer I who live, but Christ who lives in me" (Gal 2:20). On the other hand, this identification between Paul's "I" and Christ is also a relationship of faith and love. The apostle goes on to say that "the life I now live in the flesh I live by faith in the Son of God, who loved me and gave himself for me" (Gal 2:20).

Identification with Christ, therefore, leads the Christian to a clear goal, which is summarized by the eighteenth-century Italian moral theologian and doctor of the church, St. Alphonsus Liguori: "The sanctity and perfection of a soul consists entirely in loving Jesus Christ, our God, our sovereign good, and our Redeemer." All of the many and varied practices of the Christian life are oriented toward this goal—for example, the pious reception of the sacraments, the reading of and meditation on Sacred Scripture and in particular the New Testament, the recitation of and meditation on the mysteries of the Rosary, the spirit of mortification and penance, the practice of the virtues in work and daily life, and active participation in the Church's evangelizing mission.

The Holy Spirit in the Life of the Christian

As we saw in chapter three, the Holy Spirit is the love between the Father and the Son which is eternally present within the Trinity. Sacred Scripture particularly associates this Third Divine Person with grace, which is the overflow of God's own eternal love toward us. This revealed truth, like those truths which regard the Father and the Son, has meaningful consequences for the Christian's daily life.

In the Nicene Creed, Christians profess their faith in the Father, the Son, and the Holy Spirit; the third divine Person is recognized as "the Lord, the giver of life." These words from the profession of faith invite the Christian to recognize the special action by which, as we also saw in chapter three, the Paraclete operates to communicate to man the Redemption carried out by Christ. The Holy Spirit is the one at work in bringing about the Christian's identification with Christ and in guiding this identification to its fulfillment. In line with the testimony of the New Testament, the Fathers of the Church perceived the action of the Holy Spirit in enlightening, purifying, and strengthening the Christian so as to live in accord with the new identity he has received, an identity which also comes from the same Paraclete.

In light of these truths, we might ask: Why would the Christian need to specifically invoke the Holy Spirit? Might it be enough to simply address the Father and profess faith in

Christ? We can answer these questions by, first of all, looking to lived Christian experience. In the fourth century, St. Basil—a theologian and later bishop who lived in present-day Turkey—wrote the treatise *On the Holy Spirit* to defend the Christian worship of the Holy Spirit, along with the Father and the Son. Basil recalls that Christ commanded his disciples to baptize "in the name of the Father and of the Son and of the Holy Spirit" (Mt 28:19). This doctor of the church adamantly states that the invocation of the third divine Person is an essential part of the adoration of the true God. He gives his admonishment "to every man that sets aside the Spirit, that his faith in the Father and the Son will be useless, for he cannot even hold it without the presence of the Spirit."

In view of this teaching and of our study of the Paraclete, we can reflect on the role of the Holy Spirit in Christian life. Through baptism, the Christian is inserted not simply into "God," in a general sense, but into the very life of the Trinity. He becomes an adopted son through Jesus Christ. Through this new communion, the Christian is called to live out a personal relationship in which he addresses the Father with filial confidence, the Son within a communion of faith and love, and also to recognize the Holy Spirit as the divine Person who leads him into the Trinitarian communion.

Hence, if we were to ignore the Holy Spirit, we would be missing an essential part of God's revelation: that the Holy Spirit is a *person*, along with the Father and the Son, with whom we are called to develop a close personal relationship, like that intimacy which we are also called to live with the Father and the Son.

The Christian needs to respond to grace so as to make this relationship with the Holy Spirit a living and vital reality. As in the case of the "sense" of God's fatherly love and that of

Christ's closeness, St. Josemaría Escrivá notes that the Christian should come to "grasp" the truth of the Paraclete's presence. In one of the points of meditation in his book *The Forge,* he addresses the Christian who has come to this realization: "Now you feel his Love within you, and you want to talk to him, to be his friend, to confide in him."

Over the centuries, the Church has expressed her supernatural instinct to pray to the Holy Spirit in various ways, which include frequent invocation in the liturgy and in vocal prayer. A prime example is the medieval hymn "Veni, Creator Spiritus," traditionally attributed to the ninth-century German monk Rabanus Maurus. This canticle powerfully evokes the way the Holy Spirit directs and strengthens all our actions and leads us ever more deeply into the Trinitarian communion. The hymn addresses the third divine Person with these words: "Through thee may we the Father know, / Through thee, the eternal Son, / And thee, the Spirit of them both, / Thrice-blessed Three in one."

In addition to these specific invocations, the Christian spiritual tradition encourages the more fundamental attitude of *docility* to the Holy Spirit. This docility implies a trusting and faith-filled openness of soul to the multiform action of the Paraclete. Such a disposition is a condition for the full development of the life of grace.

With our reference to the Holy Spirit, we can bring a close to our description of the Trinitarian aspects present in the Christian's life of grace. While this action is certainly extraordinary and supernatural, the fruit of God's special action, it also manifests the Christian's correspondence or response to grace. In all of this activity, grace does not lead us away from those realities which are given to us through nature. As we saw in chapter one, God's supernatural action does not take away our nature but elevates it and leads it to the fulfillment God desires. Grace leads us to recognize the will of God precisely in those human realities, even the most ordinary and everyday ones, which have been elevated to God through Christ.

The Blessed Virgin Mary as Model and Mediatrix for the Christian

Our reflection on grace in the Christian life has a key reference point in the Blessed Virgin Mary. In her life, we see in a maximum yet concrete way God's plan for the action of grace in the human person. At the Annunciation, the angel Gabriel greets her with the Greek word *kecharitomene*, "full of grace" (Lk 1:28), which can also be translated as "crowned with favor." Catholic theology has seen these words as an expression of the special divine favor and superabundant graces that God bestowed upon Mary, in light of her intimate connection with God's plan of salvation.

God's special gifts to Mary are a sign of the special graces which God desires to grant to his people and to all of mankind. The greetings of the archangel Gabriel—"Hail, full of grace, the Lord is with you!"—fulfill the divine promises that God would make his dwelling among his people in his holy city (Zep 3:14; Zec 9:9). John Paul II observes that the words "full of grace" have an echo in the "blessing" spoken of by Paul in the Letter to the Ephesians. The apostle notes that God the Father has blessed Christians "in Christ with every spiritual blessing in the heavenly places." Christians, the apostle goes on to note, have been chosen by God "before the foundation of the world, that we should be holy and blameless before him" (Eph 1:3–4). Through Christ, as the Polish pontiff comments, a "fullness" of grace has been granted to all mankind. At the same time, as John Paul II goes on to say, God has wanted this blessing in Jesus Christ to refer to Mary "in a special and exceptional degree."

The Blessed Virgin Mary thus manifests God's free and gratuitous decision to raise all people to the divine life. In addition, Mary's life shows, also in a maximum way, the manner in which grace arouses the free response of the creature. The Second Vatican Council notes that, in a singular way, Mary "cooperated by her obedience, faith, hope and burning charity in the work of the Saviour in giving back supernatural life to souls." In Mary, assumed body and soul into heaven and crowned as Queen of heaven and earth, "the Church has already reached"—the Council states—"that perfection whereby she is without spot or wrinkle." Because she continues to exercise her motherly care through her maternal intercession in heaven, the Church honors her as mediatrix of grace. The Christian faithful, meditating on her example and turning to her motherly help, move toward that same perfection. In this way, they allow God's grace to work fully within them.

The Progress and Culmination of the Spiritual Life

Perhaps, in light of the truths about God's free gift of grace, we might be tempted to ask: Why is it that the Christian needs to struggle? Why talk about spiritual battle? The *Catechism of the Catholic Church* in fact reminds us that a "spiritual battle" is necessary if we want to "act habitually according to the Spirit of Christ."

To resolve such a dilemma, as the Irish theologian Paul O'Callaghan points out, we can recall that "grace received is none other than the life of Christ in the believer." Grace, he observes, elevates human nature and reproduces in each person the stages of the life of Jesus Christ on earth. Christ's life, while being full of grace and truth (Jn 1:17), was a life of struggle: of obedience, intense work, humble service, patience in the midst of opposition, and finally intense suffering and death on the Cross. In this life, we see how, as we explained in chapters eight and nine, grace seeks to energize the free and generous cooperation of the person.

When this cooperation comes about, we can speak of authentic *progress* in the spiritual life. As we noted in chapter eight, the Christian's good works can bring about an increase in grace and eternal life. This growth in grace is not the same as growth in human virtue. While human virtues grow by our own human efforts, the growth in the life of grace remains always a free gift granted by God. Progress in the spiritual life is never about trying to get closer to God by our own efforts. Nonetheless, in his benevolence, God has promised to grant us an increase in grace in response to our cooperation with grace. This growth is never simply "individual": spiritual progress redounds in benefit to the other members of the Church, to whom the Christian is united in one body (1 Cor 12:12), and to the entire world, for whom the Church is a sign and means of salvation.

The presence of sanctifying grace in the soul—as we have seen in chapter six—involves a participation in God's life in all of our being, and not just in certain capacities of the person. Hence, progress in grace is different from growth in a particular virtue. By progress in grace, the person's whole being comes to a deeper participation in the life of God. In doing so, the Christian follows the example of Jesus Christ himself, who in his humanity "advanced in wisdom, and age, and grace with God and men" (Lk 2:52, Douay-Rheims translation).

At the same time, this more general increase in grace also leads—again, by God's gift—to a greater capacity to live the theological virtues of faith, hope, and love, as well as a new strength to live the human virtues. The person's will becomes ever more conformed to the will of God, more consistent in seeking the good, and grace corrects the disordered tendencies of the soul.

Our cooperation with grace, with its corresponding spiritual progress, can occur in myriad ways: through the reception of the sacraments with proper dispositions, by means of faithfulness to the practices of Christian piety, and by the exercise of charity within the duties of our state in life. Each one of these actions, in different ways, brings the Christian to a deeper communion with God, and also shapes our character so that we might become more profoundly identified with Christ. For example, through the practice of spiritual reading we can enrich our mind with the truths of God and the spiritual life, thus enabling us to grow in prudence as well as in other virtues. Through the practice of mental prayer, the Christian can develop, in an affective manner, that personal relationship with God which began with baptism.

Along with this potential to cooperate with grace, we should also note that if such cooperation is lacking, progress in the spiritual life will also be lacking, and we run the risk of diminishing or losing the presence of grace as well as the virtues. Such a state might not necessarily involve the complete loss of grace, as in the case of mortal sin, but rather might be symptomatic of the condition known as *lukewarmness*. Lukewarmness is not specifically an action or sin, but rather a state of the soul marked by a diminishing love of God. A person in such a state usually falls into deliberate venial sins, to which he has become indifferent. The lukewarm person might still remain in the state of grace and hence retain friendship with God. At the same time, such a person's interior dispositions are not in harmony with the grace God has infused into his soul. The lukewarm person risks falling, sooner or later, into mortal sin and into serious unfaithfulness to his commitments to God and others.

Numerous authorities on the spiritual life, down through the centuries, have distinguished three stages in spiritual progress: the *purgative* phase in which the Christian struggles to detach himself from sin; the *illuminative* stage in which God enlightens the soul to live according to faith and charity; and finally the *contemplative* phase in which the believer reaches a superior level of union with God.

While these stages of the spiritual life reflect important elements of the way the Christian grows in grace, we should avoid seeing them too rigidly. The spiritual life, since it is the action of God in each individual, will always go beyond strict categories. Thomas Aquinas recognized that, while grace can grow in the soul and restore the damage done by sin, this action will never be complete in this life. There will always remain a certain tendency to sin, and the believer will always retain the capacity to reject God.

Consequently, the full unfolding of grace in the soul will only occur in the next life. Grace is the beginning of a genuine participation in God's life, but it is also like a seed (see Mt 13:31) which is meant to develop into something far greater. John reminds Christians that "we are God's children now," yet he also states that the true meaning of this identity remains to be seen: "It does not yet appear what we shall be, but we know that when he appears we shall be like him, for we shall see him as he is" (1 Jn 3:2).

In the resurrection of the dead and in the "new heaven" and "new earth" (Rev 21:1) which Christians await, the action of grace will reach its fulfillment in man and all creation. As the Second Vatican Council affirmed, death will be overcome and "the sons of God will be raised up in Christ, and what was sown in weakness and corruption will be invested with incorruptibility."

The blessedness of this transformed world, the Council continues, "will answer and surpass all the longings for peace which spring up in the human heart." The grace of God continually inspires Christians to struggle against sin and carry out the good, with the confidence that grace will also bring these efforts to their full realization.

Sources

Abbreviations

AH Peter Brown. *Augustine of Hippo: A Biography*. 2nd ed. Berkeley: University of California Press, 2000. 1st ed., 1967.

AT Juan Luis Lorda. *Antropología Teológica*. Pamplona, Spain: Ediciones Universidad de Navarra, 2009.

BD Franco Montanari, ed. *The Brill Dictionary of Ancient Greek*. Online edition, 2015; last updated, 2018.

CBD Scott Hahn, ed. *Catholic Bible Dictionary*. New York: Doubleday, 2009.

CCC *Catechism of the Catholic Church*. Washington, DC: Libreria Editrice Vaticana and United States Conference of Catholic Bishops, 1994.

CG Paul O'Callaghan. *Children of God in the World: An Introduction to Theological Anthropology*. Washington, DC: The Catholic University of America Press, 2016.

DBT Xavier Leon-Dufour, ed. *Dictionary of Biblical Theology*. 2nd ed. Boston: St. Paul, 1995.

DUT Lucas Francisco Mateo-Seco. *Dios Uno y Trino*. 3rd ed. Pamplona, Spain: Ediciones Universidad de Navarra, S.A., 2008.

DG Rebecca Harden Weaver. *Divine Grace and Human Agency: A Study of the Semi-Pelagian Controversy*. Macon, GA: Mercer University Press, 1996.

DJ Council of Trent. Decree on Justification (January 13, 1547). In *Decrees of the Ecumenical Councils*, vol. 2, *Trent to Vatican II*. Edited by Norman Tanner. London: Sheed and Ward, 1990, 671–683.

DV John Paul II. Encyclical on the Holy Spirit *Dominum et Vivificantem* (May 18, 1986). Vatican website: www.vatican.va.

EG Johann Auer. *El Evangelio de la Gracia*. Translated by Claudio Gancho. Barcelona, Spain: Herder, 1982.

GC Jose Antonio Sayes. *La Gracia de Cristo*. Madrid, Spain: Biblioteca de Autores Cristianos, 1993.

  GS Vatican Council II. Pastoral Constitution on the Church in the Modern World *Gaudium et Spes* (December 7, 1965). Vatican website: www.vatican.va.

 JBC Raymond E. Brown et al., eds. *The Jerome Biblical Commentary.* Englewood Cliffs, NJ: Prentice-Hall, 1968.

  LG Vatican Council II. Dogmatic Constitution on the Church *Lumen Gentium* (November 21, 1964). Vatican website: www.vatican.va.

  OT Old Testament.

 NCE *New Catholic Encyclopedia.* 2nd ed. 15 vols. Detroit: Gale, 2003; Gale eBooks.

  NT New Testament.

  NG Mattias Joseph Scheeben. *Nature and Grace.* Translated by Cyril Vollert. St. Louis, MO: B. Herder, 1954.

  ST Thomas Aquinas. *Summa Theologiae.* Translated by Fathers of the English Dominican Province. 2nd ed. Online edition at New Advent, edited by Kevin Knight, 2017; 1st ed. 1920.

TDNT Gerhard Kittel and Gerhard Friedrich, eds. *Theological Dictionary of the New Testament.* 10 vols. Translated and edited by Geoffrey W. Bromiley. Grand Rapids: Wm. B. Eerdmans, 1967; reprinted 1995.

  TE José Luis Illanes. *Tratado de Teología Espiritual.* Rev. 3rd ed. Pamplona, Spain: Ediciones Universidad de Navarra S.A., 2011; 1st ed., 2007.

Introduction

"fully reveals": *GS*, no. 22.

"his weakness," "deep wonder": John Paul II, Encyclical Letter on the Redeemer of Man *Redemptor Hominis* (March 4, 1979), no. 10, Vatican website: www.vatican.va.

Chapter 1. Man's Calling to Communion with God

Man's Ultimate Purpose: To Participate in the Inner Life of God

"The root reason": *GS*, no. 19.

"Man would not": *GS*, no. 19.

On man's longing for something more than material things, see Jutta Burggraf, *Made for Freedom: Loving, Defending and Living God's Gift* (New Rochelle, NY: Scepter, 2012), pp. 48–49.

For Aquinas on the intellect's desire to know God, see *ST* 1.12.1.

On the definition of the will, see John A. Hardon, *Modern Catholic Dictionary* (Garden City, NY: Doubleday, 1980), s.v. "Will."

"by its very nature": Burggraf, *Made for Freedom*, p. 48.

On the ancient cyclical view of time, see John Jamieson Carswell Smart, Arnold Joseph Toynbee, and William Markowitz, "Time," in *Encyclopedia Britannica*, online ed., accessed November 2022, https://www.britannica.com/science/time.

Regarding the OT sense of time, see P. C. Berg, "Time (in the Old Testament)," in *NCE*, vol. 14, p. 83.

On the Greek words for time, see s.vv. "χρόνος" and "καιρός" in *BD*.

"we mustn't squander": from Josemaría Escrivá, *Friends of God* (London: Scepter, 1981), no. 39.

The Natural and Supernatural Orders

On the origin of the word *nature* or *natural*, see *NG*, pp. 19–20.

On the meaning of *nature*, see also Hardon, s.v. "nature"; and also *AT*, p. 135.

On the meaning of *supernatural*, see *NG*, p. 25.

"A transfiguration": *NG*, p. 11.

For discussion of Christ as the New Adam, see *CCC*, no. 504.

On the new creation, see Lucien Cerfaux, *Christ in the Theology of St. Paul*, trans. Geoffrey Webb and Adrian Walker (New York: Herder and Herder, 1959), pp. 339–340.

For the extremes of Pelagianism and Lutheranism/Jansenism, see *NG*, p. 1.

On the use of the use of *natural* and *supernatural* to express the condition of man, see *NG*, p. 2.

On Cajetan's position on pure nature, see *CG*, p. 396; and Rupert Johannes Mayer, "Man Is Inclined to His Last End by Nature, though He Cannot Reach It by Nature but Only by Grace: The Principle of the Debate about Nature and Grace in Thomas Aquinas, Thomism and Henri de Lubac. A Response to Lawrence Feingold," *Angelicum* 88, no. 4 (2011): 895–901.

"Aquinas does indeed hold": *ST* 1.62.1.

On the natural end of human nature in Aquinas, see Mayer, pp. 889–890.

"the ultimate end of man's nature is the perfect vision of God, only accessible with the help of God": see *ST* 1-2.5.5.

On de Lubac's rejection of a purely natural end, see Mayer, pp. 901–902; see also *CG*, p. 398.

On Pius XII's teaching on the gratuity of the supernatural order, see the Encyclical on the Human Race *Humani Generis* (August 12, 1950), no. 26, Vatican website: www.vatican.va.

"the ultimate vocation": *GS*, no. 22.

The Incarnation of the Word Sheds Light on Man and History

"The Lord is the goal": *GS*, no. 45.

For the teaching of Vatican I regarding divine revelation, see Dogmatic Constitution on the Catholic Faith *Dei Filius* (April 24, 1870), Interdisciplinary Encyclopedia of Religion & Science, https://inters.org/Vatican-Council-I-Dei-Filius; original Latin text in H. Denzinger, *Enchiridion Symbolorum, Definitionum et Declarationum de Rebus Fidei et Morum*, ed. P. Hünermann (Freiburg im Breisgau: Herder, 1991), 3001–3020, English trans. by *Welcome to the Catholic Church*, Harmony Media.

Predestination and the Vocation of Man

On Christ's humanity as a reflection of the divine nature, see *CG*, p. 69.

"[Christ] blazed a trail": *GS*, no. 22.

On the meaning of *predestine*, see K. L. Schmidt, s.vv. "ὁρίζω," and "προορίζω," in *TDNT*, vol. 5, p. 452 and Fernand Prat, *The Theology of St. Paul*, vol. 2, trans. John L. Stoddard (Westminster, MD: Newman, 1950), p. 87.

On the meaning of *predestination*, see *CG*, pp. 129–130.

On the meaning of vocation as involving human freedom, and on the end of the vocation, see Fernand Prat, *The Theology of St. Paul*, vol. 1, trans. John L. Stoddard (Westminster, MD: Newman, 1926), p. 436.

Regarding the special grace of vocation, see *TE*, pp. 182–184.

"has the surprising capacity": John Paul II, General Audience (November 23, 1983), Vatican website: www.vatican.va; translation from the Italian is my own.

"your human vocation," "That is the reason": Josemaría Escrivá, *Christ Is Passing By* (New York: Scepter, 1974), no. 46.

Chapter 2. The Meaning of Grace

Hymn "Amazing Grace," by John Newton (1972), https://www.hymnal.net/en/hymn/h/313.

For Lorda's description of the broadest sense of grace, see *AT*, p. 374.

For background on the word *charis*, see *TDNT*, vol. 9, pp. 373–374.

Grace in the Old Testament

On *hen*, see Walther Zimmerli, "Χάϱις. B. The Old Testament," in *TDNT*, vol. 9, pp. 376–377.

Regarding the novelty of the revelation of God in Ex 34:6, see Leon R. Kass, *Founding God's Nation: Reading Exodus* (New Haven: Yale University Press, 2021), pp. 562–563.

Regarding *rahum*, see Rudolf Bultmann, "ἔλεος. B. The OT and Jewish Usage," in *TDNT*, vol. 2, pp. 480–481; see also Jules Cambier and Xavier Léon-Dufour, "Mercy," trans. Thomas M. Spittler, in *DBT*, p. 351.

Regarding the way *hen* remains in man, see Zimmerli, "Χάϱις," p. 380.

Regarding the meaning of *hesed*, see *TDNT*, vol. 2, pp. 479–480.

On *emet*, see Jacques Guillet, "Grace," trans. William J. Young, in *DBT*, 218; see also *GC*, p. 14, and Ignace de la Potterie, "Truth," trans. Donald F. Brezine, in *DBT*, pp. 618–619.

"in a plan": see *CCC*, no. 1.

Regarding the overview of grace in the Old Testament, see *GC*, pp. 10–13.

Regarding the distinction between the Old and New Testament visions of grace, see *EG*, pp. 25–28, esp. p. 28.

Grace in the New Testament

On the novelty of grace in the New Testament, see Hans Conzelmann, "Χάϱις κτλ. D. New Testament," in *TDNT*, vol. 9, p. 391.

On the use of grace in the theological writings apart from Paul, see *GC*, pp. 15–17 and Conzelmann, "Χάϱις κτλ. D. New Testament," in *TDNT*, vol. 9, p. 391.

On the understanding of *charis* in the Greek world at Jesus' time, see Hans Conzelmann, "Χάϱις κτλ. A. Profane Greek," in *TDNT*, vol. 9, pp. 375–376.

Regarding Eph 2:4–5, see commentary on Eph 2:8–10 in Faculty of Theology of the University of Navarre, *The New Testament* (New York: Scepter, 2008).

On the distinct sense of the word *grace*, see *AT*, pp. 382–383.

On grace as destroying sin, see Conzelmann, "Χάϱις κτλ. D. New Testament," in *TDNT*, vol. 9, p. 395.

Regarding works as a fruit of grace, see Guillet, "Grace," in *DBT*, p. 220.

Regarding the use of *life* in John, see Rudolf Bultmann, "ζωή. E. The Concept of Life in the NT," in *TDNT*, vol. 2, p. 870.

On the contrast between *zoe* and *bios*, see "ζωή. A. ζωή in Greek Usage," in *TDNT*, vol. 2, pp. 835–837.

On grace as eternal life in John, see *GC*, pp. 20–22 and *CG*, pp. 133–134.

Dimensions of the Life of Grace

On created grace, see *ST* 1-2.110.2.

On the meaning of justification, see *AT*, p. 452.

On the distinction between healing grace and elevating grace, see *CG*, pp. 133, 300; and Joseph Pohle, "Actual Grace," in Charles Herbermann et al., *The Catholic Encyclopedia*, vol. 6 (New York: Encyclopedia Press, 1913; online ed. at New Advent, ed. Kevin Knight).

On the grace of specific sacraments, see the following paragraphs of *CCC*: baptism, 1265; Eucharist, 1391; confirmation, 1302–1303; penance, 1468; holy orders, 1585; matrimony, 1661; anointing of the sick, 1520.

"are efficacious signs": see *CCC*, no. 1131.

On grace in Christ, see *ST* 3.7.1.

On Mary as full of grace and the interpretation of de la Potterie, see commentary in Juan Luis Bastero, *Mary, Mother of the Redeemer: A Mariology Textbook*, trans. Michael Adams and Philip Griffin (Portland, OR: Four Courts, 2006), pp. 106–108; Bastero cites Ignace de la Potterie, "Κεχαριτωμένη En Lc 1,28 Étude Philologique," *Biblica* 68, no. 3 (1987), pp. 357–382, and Ignace de la Potterie, "Κεχαριτωμένη En Lc 1,28 Étude Exégétique et Théologique," *Biblica* 68, no. 4 (1987), pp. 480–508.

On Mary's mediating function, see *LG*, nos. 60–62.

"she is our mother": *LG*, no. 61.

Chapter 3. Grace as Indwelling of the Holy Spirit

The Holy Spirit as Uncreated Gift

On Bernini's *Chair of St. Peter*, see Howard Hibbard, "Gian Lorenzo Bernini," *Encyclopedia Britannica*, online ed., accessed December 8, 2021.

On Lombard's position regarding Rom 5:5 and the medieval debate regarding this interpretation, see *AT*, pp. 430–431.

For Aquinas on God as the source of man's sharing in the divine life, see *ST* 1.38.1.

On the procession of the Holy Spirit, see *DUT*, pp. 522, 527.

On the Greek word for procession, see "ἐκπορεύω," in *BD*.

Regarding Aquinas on love as a specific way of describing the Holy Spirit's procession, see *ST* 1.27.4.

On the relationship between gift and love, see *ST* 1.38.2.

The Holy Spirit as Gift of God to Man in the Old Testament

Regarding the Hebrew word for *spirit*, see Werner Bieder, "B. Spirit in the OT," in *TDNT*, vol. 6, p. 360.

On John Paul II's commentary on Gen 1:2, see *DV*, no. 12.

Regarding the spirit in Ez 36:26–27, see Bieder, "Spirit," p. 360.

Apropos of the action of the Holy Spirit as interior force in key persons in the Old Testament, see commentary on Is 11:1–9 in Faculty of Theology of the University of Navarre, *The Navarre Bible: The Pentateuch*, trans. Michael Adams (Princeton, NJ: Scepter, 1999).

Regarding the significance of Nm 11:29 see commentary on Jl 3:1–5 in Faculty of Theology of the University of Navarre, *The Navarre Bible: Minor Prophets*, trans. Michael Adams (New York: Scepter, 2017).

On the presence of God in the pillar of cloud, see Ex 33:9; on this presence in the tabernacle, see Ex 40:34; on this presence in the temple, see 1 Kgs 9:3; on this topic and the development of God's presence to his people, see *GC*, pp. 268–269.

The Promise and Gift of the Spirit in the New Testament

On the presence of God in the tent of meeting, see Ex 40:34.

The literal Greek meaning of *dwelt* comes from "σκηνόω," in *BD*.

On Mary as the New Tabernacle, see Jean Galot, *Mary in the Gospel* (Westminster, MD: Newman, 1965), pp. 57–59.

On the significance of the ark of covenant, see "ark of covenant," in *CBD*.

Regarding John Paul II's teaching on the relationship between the Last Supper and the gift of the Holy Spirit, see *DV*, no. 23.

"this Redemption is, at the same time": *DV*, no. 24.

Commentary on the Greek word *Parakleton* draws from Johannes Behm, "παράκλητος," in *TDNT*, vol. 5, pp. 800–804.

For Augustine's commentary on the Holy Spirit as love, see Augustine, *On the Trinity*, bk. 15, chap. 17, no. 31; analysis here also draws from *DUT*, pp. 569–570.

"in the Holy Spirit": *DV*, no. 10.

The Holy Spirit's Presence and the Indwelling of the Trinity in the Soul

With respect to the scriptural context for the indwelling, see *CG*, pp. 281–282.

On the life of the Christian in Christ Jesus, see *GC*, pp. 275–276.

For Aquinas' view on the mode of presence of the Trinity in the soul through grace, see *ST* 1.43.3.

For Aquinas' view of the presence of the Holy Trinity through the acts of wisdom and love, see Thomas Aquinas, *Summa Contra Gentiles, Book Four: Salvation*, trans. Charles J. O'Neill (Notre Dame, IN: University of Notre Dame Press, 1975; 1st ed., Hanover House, 1957), chap. 21, no. 2; on the Son as Wisdom, see chap. 12.

For commentary on the position of Aquinas on the inhabitation of the Trinity, see *GC*, pp. 293–298 and *AT*, pp. 441–442.

Regarding the "light of glory" as a way of understanding the indwelling of the Trinity, see *AT*, p. 443, and *GC*, pp. 296–297. Aquinas speaks of the light of glory in *ST* 1.12.2.

"only in degree": Leo XIII, Encyclical on the Holy Spirit *Divinum Illud Munus* (May 9, 1897), no. 9, Vatican website: www.vatican.va.

Reference to Pius XII's teaching is from his Encyclical on the Mystical Body of Christ *Mystici Corporis Christi* (June 29, 1943), nos. 78–79, Vatican website: www.vatican.va; commentary found in *AT*, p. 443.

"human life becomes permeated": *DV*, no. 52.

"The Spirit dwells," "prays on their behalf," "makes the Church": *LG*, no. 4.

Scriptural context and definition of *charism* draws from Augustin George and Pierre Grelot, "Charisms," trans. Patrick J. Boyle, in *DBT*, pp. 68–69; see also *LG*, no. 12.

The Presence of the Holy Spirit and the "Divinization" of Man

On man's participation in the divine nature without a divinization in the strict sense, and for background on the Fathers on divinization, see David Vincent Meconi, "Divinization (Theosis), Doctrine of," in *New Catholic Encyclopedia*, Supplement 2010, ed. Robert L. Fastiggi (Detroit, MI: Gale, 2010; Gale eBooks), vol. 1, p. 410.

Regarding the way Christians are truly divinized, see *AT*, pp. 411–413.

"assumed humanity": Athanasius, *On the Incarnation* (Crestwood, NY: St. Vladimir's Seminary, 2011), chap. 54, no. 3.

"Let us rejoice": Augustine, *Lectures or Tractates on the Gospel According to St. John*, trans. John Gibb and James Innes, in Philip Schaff, ed., *Nicene and Post-Nicene Fathers*, series 1, vol. 7 (Peabody, MA: Hendrickson, 1995; 1st ed., Christian Literature Publishing Company, 1888), chap. 21, no. 8.

On the distinction between the Eastern view of divinization and the notion of grace, see *AT*, p. 374; on the mystical element present in the Eastern tradition, see *AT*, pp. 413–417.

"perceive that one": John Paul II, Apostolic Letter on the Centenary of *Orientalium Dignitas Orientale Lumen* (May 2, 1995), no. 16, Vatican website: www.vatican.va.

Chapter 4. Grace as Divine Filiation in Christ

God as Father in the Old Testament

On divine filiation as the end of the mystery of salvation, see *AT*, p. 391.

Regarding the ancient use of *father* in religion, the Hindu god Dyaus, and Zeus, see Gottlob Schrenk, "πατήρ. A. The Father Concept in the Indo-European World and Graeco-Roman Antiquity," in *TDNT*, vol. 5, pp. 952–953.

On *Dyaus* and this word as the root for terms for God, see David Leeming, *A Dictionary of Asian Mythology* (Oxford University Press, online ed., 2002).

On the significance of the title for God in Ex 3:14, see *CCC*, no. 206.

Regarding the sense of God's holiness, as seen in Lv 11:44, see *DUT*, p. 58.

On the use of *father* in the Old Testament, see Gottfried Quell, "πατήρ. B. The Father Concept in the Old Testament," in *TDNT*, vol. 5, pp. 961, 965, 970–971; "only comparatively sparing use" comes from the same work, p. 965; see also *CG*, pp. 251–252.

On God's showing himself to be a father in the Old Testament and the notion of the just man and king as son of God, see "Fathers and Father," in *DBT*, pp. 171–172.

On God the father as not being the dominant image for God in the Old Testament, see *CG*, p. 251 and *AT*, p. 392, in addition to the Quell citation above.

God as Father in the New Testament

Regarding the differences in the term *father* as applied to God in the Old and New Testaments, see *CG*, pp. 250, 255.

On the centrality and significance of the New Testament's teaching on God the Father, see *DUT*, pp. 110–111, and *AT*, p. 392.

On the collective sense of God's fatherly role in the Old Testament, see *CG*, p. 252.

On Jesus' union with the Father, see *DUT*, p. 112; on the significance of *Abba*, see Gottlob Schrenk and Gottfried Quell, "πατήρ. Father in the New Testament," in *TDNT*, vol. 5, p. 985.

Regarding Mt 11:27 and Christ's claim to go beyond the Law and the Prophets, see commentary in John L. McKenzie, "The Gospel According to Matthew," in *JBC*, vol. 2.

On the special meaning of *Father* in the fourth Gospel, and the relationship of dependence between the Father and the Son, see Shrenk and Quell, "πατήρ. Father in the New Testament," pp. 997–998.

On the eternal generation of the Father, see *DUT*, pp. 546–547 and *ST* 1.27.2.

Grace as Participation in the Filiation of Christ, in the Holy Spirit

"at the price": *DV*, no. 14.

Commentary on Fathers of the Church draws from *AT*, pp. 397, 399–400.

St. Irenaeus of Lyons' teaching can be found in *Against Heresies* (Middletown, DE: Aeterna, 2016; reprint of Wm. B. Eerdmans, 2001), bk. 3, chap. 19, no. 1.

Text of St. Cyril of Jerusalem is in *Catechetical Lectures*, trans. Edwin Hamilton Gifford, in Philip Schaff and Henry Wace, eds., *Nicene and Post-Nicene Fathers*, series 2, vol. 7 (Buffalo: Christian Literature, 1894; online ed. at New Advent, ed. Kevin Knight), lecture 21, no. 1; Cyril's text on the Eucharist is in lecture 22 of the same work.

"certain participation of natural sonship": *ST* 3.3.5.

Regarding the notion of participation in Aquinas, see Melissa Eitenmiller, "Grace as Participation According to St. Thomas Aquinas," in *New Blackfriars* 98, no. 1078 (November 2017): pp. 692–693, 697–698.

On man being introduced into the Trinity, see Fernando Ocáriz, *Naturaleza, Gracia, y Gloria*, 2nd ed. (Pamplona, Spain: Ediciones Universidad de Navarra, S.A., 2001), pp. 72–77.

Regarding the personal mode of knowledge of love made possible by grace, see *ST* 1.43.3.

On the concept of adoption, see *ST* 3.23.1., art. 1; and Ocáriz, *Naturaleza*, pp. 74–75.

Divine Filiation in the Spiritual Tradition

For background regarding divine filiation in Aquinas, Scheeben, Marmion, St. Thérèse, and St. Josemaría, see Ernst Burkhart and Javier López, *Ordinary Life and Holiness in the Teaching of St. Josemaría: A Study in Spiritual Theology*, trans. Javier del Castillo, vol. 2 (New York: Scepter, 2020; original Spanish version, Madrid: Rialp, 2011), pp. 48, 50–53; regarding the experience of October 16, 1931, see p. 13–18 of this work; the summary of St. Josemaría's teaching on divine filiation draws from chapter 4 of this work, pp. 9–135.

On divine filiation in the liturgy, see *AT*, p. 402, and E. J. Gratsch, "Doxology, Liturgical," in *NCE*, vol. 4, pp. 890–891.

Divine Filiation, Belonging to the Church, and Human Fraternity

Regarding the Church as brethren in Christ and family of God, see *LG*, nos. 2, 6.

"a people made one": *LG*, no. 4; the Council cites Cyprian, *On the Lord's Prayer*, no. 23.

"the Church is in Christ": *LG*, no. 1.

"faith has untold power"; "Christ shed": Pope Francis, Encyclical Letter on Fraternity and Social Friendship *Fratelli Tutti* (October 3, 2020), no. 85; citation in first quote is from Pope John Paul II, Message to the Handicapped at Angelus in Osnabrück, Germany (November 16, 1980).

Chapter 5. Grace as Forgiveness from God: Justification

Regarding the translation of *righteousness* as *justice* in Rom 3:22, see "δῐ̆καιοσυˇ́νη" in *BD*.

Justification in the Old Testament

Regarding the specific meaning of justice for the Chosen People, see *GC*, p. 186; regarding this topic and the relation with the Greek sense of justice, see *EG*, p. 120.

On God as the source of law, and for commentary on Dt 32:4, see Gottfried Quell, "δίκη. The Concept of Law in the OT," in *TDNT*, vol. 2, p. 176.

On the justice of God in relation to the covenant, see *GC*, p. 187.

On God as ruler and God's action as a consequence of justice, see Quell, "δίκη," pp. 176–177.

On the notion of justice and its connection with grace, see *GC*, p. 188; this work cites Friedrich Nötscher, "*Justicia*," in J. B. Bauer, *Diccionario de Teología Bíblica* (Barcelona: Herder, 1967).

Regarding justification in the Old Testament, see *GC*, p. 188; this work in turn cites Walther Eichrodt, *Theology of the Old Testament* (English ed., Philadelphia: Westminster, 1961), vol. 1.

Regarding the Hebrew root for the *righteous*, see Joseph Samuel C. F. Frey, *A Hebrew, Latin, and English Dictionary* (London: Hamilton, 1819), vol. 2, p. 1147.

On justice as interior submission to the law, see *AT*, p. 453.

Justification in the New Testament

On justice as an interior reality in the NT, see *GC*, p. 139.

The Greek word for *righteousness* in 1 Cor 1:30 is δικαιοσύνη; see entry for this term in *BD*.

On the resonances of "grace and truth" with *emet* and *hesed*, see commentary on Jn 1:17 in Bruce Vawter, "The Gospel According to John," in *JBC*, vol. 2.

On the relation between *emet*, *hesed*, and justice in the Old Testament, see *GC*, p. 189.

On the context to the Letter to the Romans, see "Introduction to *Roman: 3:* Message," in Faculty of Theology of the University of Navarre, *The Navarre Bible: The New Testament* (New York: Scepter, 2008), pp. 563–564.

Regarding the term *emunah*, see commentary on Hb 2:1–4, in Richard T. A. Murphy, "Habakkuk," in *JBC*, vol. 1.

On faith according to Paul as a response of the whole person, see *GC*, n. 196.

Regarding the "law of sin," see "sin" in *CBD*.

Regarding the defeat of the law of sin and death, see Fernand Prat, *The Theology of St. Paul*, vol. 2, trans. John L. Stoddard (Westminster, MD: Newman, 1950), p. 222; for the Council of Trent's teaching on this, see the Council's Decree on Original Sin (June 17, 1546), in *Decrees of the Ecumenical Councils*, vol. 2, *Trent to Vatican II*, ed. Norman Tanner (London: Sheed and Ward, 1990), no. 5.

On the relationship between Paul's notion of grace and "eternal life" in John, see *GC*, pp. 140–141; on Paul's and John's respective emphases, see *CG*, pp. 132–133.

Martin Luther's View of Justification

Regarding nominalism and other cultural movements which shaped Luther, see *CG*, pp. 184–189.

On Luther's personal religious experience, see *AT*, pp. 454–455.

For Luther's description of his Tower Experience and "All at once": "An Excerpt From: *Preface to the Complete Edition of Luther's Latin Works* (1545)," trans. Andrew Thornton, OSB, Project Wittenberg, https://www.projectwittenberg.org/pub/resources/text/wittenberg/luther/tower.txt.

For Luther's teaching on faith *in nobis et sine nobis*, see *CG*, p. 192; this work cites Martin Luther, *Dr. Martin Luthers Werke: Schriften*, 6:530.

On Luther's idea of justification as a declaration, see *AT*, p. 457, and *GC*, pp. 221–222.

Regarding the aspects of Luther's vision of justification which are shared with Catholics, as well as those elements which seem incompatible with Catholic teaching and should be subject to further dialogue, see Lutheran World Federation and the Catholic Church, *Joint Declaration on the Doctrine of Justification* (1997), and *Response of the Catholic Church to the Joint Declaration of the Catholic Church and the Lutheran World Federation on the Doctrine of Justification* (1998).

On Luther's appreciation of newness of life in Christ and good works, see *CG,* p. 192.

Justification According to the Council of Trent

For the overview on the Council of Trent, see J. P. Kirsch, "Council of Trent," in *The Catholic Encyclopedia* (New York: Robert Appleton Company, 1912; online version at New Advent, ed. Kevin Knight).

"lost their innocence" and "unclean": *DJ,* chap. 1.

"was in no way": *DJ,* chap 1; see also original Latin.

"has qualified us": *DJ,* chap. 3.

"predisposing grace," "with no existing," "by giving free assent": *DJ,* chap. 5.

"the sanctification and renewal," "someone from being": *DJ,* chap. 7.

On justification as fruit of the Holy Spirit and as ingrafting into Christ, see *DJ,* chap. 7.

"are not merely": *DJ,* chap. 7.

On being further justified, see *DJ,* chap. 10.

On the need to be identified with Christ in his sufferings and glory, see *DJ,* chap. 11.

Chapter 6: Grace as Interior Transformation

On the painting of Caravaggio, see Andrew Graham-Dixon, "Caravaggio," in *Britannica Academic* (online ed., 2015).

Interior Transformation in Scripture

The Greek word for *new* in 1 Cor 5:7 is καινὴ; for the significance of this term see Johannes Behm, "καινός," in *TDNT*, vol. 3, p. 447.

On the Greek term for *regeneration*, see Friedrich Büchsel, "παλιγγενεσία," in *TDNT*, vol. 1, pp. 686–688.

Regarding *koinonia*, see the following entries in *TDNT*, vol. 3: Friedrich Hauck, "κοινός" 789–790; and "κοινωνός," 798–801, 804–807.

The Reflection on Grace during the Scholastic Period

Regarding Scholasticism in general, see "Scholasticism," in *Britannica Academic* (online ed.).

On the effort to introduce Aristotelianism to the reflection on grace, see *AT*, p. 429.

On Aristotle's notion of virtue, see Frederick Copleston, "Aristotle's Ethics," in *A History of Philosophy*, vol. 1, *Greece and Rome* (New York: Doubleday, 1993; 1st ed., 1962), pp. 334–335; see also Aristotle, *Nicomachean Ethics*, trans. Martin Ostwald (New York: Bobbs-Merrill, 1962), bk. 2, chap. 1.

Regarding Abelard's view of rectitude, see *CG*, pp. 175–176; and Kent Wallace, "Virtue and Grace in Relationship: A Theological Response to a Philosophical Account of Divinely Given Virtue," *Saint Anselm Journal* 14, no. 2 (Spring 2019), p. 49, n. 31.

On Peter Lombard's and Augustine's interpretations of Rom 5:5, see *CG*, pp. 163, 176–177.

"Now the love of God": Augustine, *On the Spirit and the Letter*, trans. Peter Holmes and Robert Ernest Wallis, ed. Benjamin B. Warfield, *Nicene and Post-Nicene Fathers*, series 1, vol. 5., ed. Philip Schaff (Buffalo: Christian Literature, 1887; online ed. at New Advent, ed. Kevin Knight), chap. 56.

Apropos of Lombard's position and the medieval reaction to it, as well as the notion of entitative and operative habits, see *AT*, pp. 431–432.

"Sanctifying grace is": see *CCC*, no. 2000.

Regarding mortal sin, see *CCC*, no. 1857.

On the possibility of recovering the state of grace, see *DJ*, chap. 14.

"at the beginning": see *CCC*, no. 2000.

Thomas Aquinas on Grace

Regarding the placement of the questions on grace in *ST*, see *AT*, p. 432.

The questions specifically dedicated to grace in *ST* are 1-2.109–114.

Regarding Aquinas' affirmation that man needs the strength of grace to act well, see *ST* 1-2.109.2.

"when a man": *ST* 1-2.110.1.

On grace as a quality of the soul in Aquinas, see *ST* 1-2.110.2.

On grace as a new state of the person, see *ST* 1-2.110.1.

"pleasing to God": *ST* 1-2.110.1, 3.

"certain forms and powers": *ST* 1-2.110.2.

"thus the movements": *ST* 1-2.110.2.

On the misunderstandings of the Catholic notion of grace and grace as not being a "thing," see *AT*, pp. 436–438.

"inheres in the soul"; "as it were": see *The Catechism of the Council of Trent*, trans. John A. McHugh and Charles J. Callan (Rockford, IL: TAN, 1923), part 2, "Third Effect Of Baptism: Grace Of Regeneration."

Grace, Virtues, and Gifts of the Holy Spirit.

Regarding the "habit" of virtues, see *GC*, p. 335 and *AT*, pp. 429–430.

On faith and its relation to the intellect, see *ST* 2-2.4.2.

On hope and its connection with the will, see *ST* 2-2.18.1, as well as *CCC*, no. 1817.

With regard to love, see *ST* 2-2.24.1.

Apropos of the infused human virtues, see *CG*, p. 334.

On the meaning of the gifts of the Holy Spirit, see *ST* 1-2.68.4.

On the basis of the seven gifts, and on Aquinas' reasoning on the sanctified man's need for the gifts, see P. F. Mulhern, "Holy Spirit, Gifts of," *NCE*, vol. 7, pp. 47–48.

On the meaning of the seven gifts, see also *CG*, pp. 338–339.

"to see with God's eyes": Pope Francis, General Audience (April 9, 2014), Vatican website: www.vatican.va.

Chapter 7: Man's Need for Grace

"finds that he": *GS*, no. 13.

On man's sinfulness and need for grace as seen in the Old Testament, see *GC*, p. 43; see also Stanislaus Lyonnet, "Sin," in *DBT*, p. 553.

On the need of the Holy Spirit to convince man of sin, see *DV*, no. 35.

For commentary on Rom 7:23, see Joseph A. Fitzmyer, "The Letter to the Romans," in *JBC*, vol. 2; see also n. 75 of this work with regard to the meaning of *I*.

On the novelty of Paul's conception of sin with regard to the OT, as well as Christ's victory over sin, see Walter Grundmann, "ἁμαρτάνω. F. Sin in the NT," in *TDNT*, vol. 1, pp. 307–311.

Regarding Jn 15:5 and its OT framework, see commentary on Jn 15:1–17 in Fitzmyer.

Pelagianism

For historical background on Pelagius and his views, see *AH*, pp. 341–342.

On the three aspects of man's action in Pelagius, see John A. Mourant and William J. Collinge, "Introduction," in *Four Anti-Pelagian Writings*, The Fathers of the Church, vol. 86 (Washington, DC: Catholic University of America Press, 1992), p. 99. Also, on Pelagius' views regarding freedom and sin, see Eugene TeSelle, "The Background: Augustine and the Pelagian Controversy," in *Grace for Grace*, ed. Alexander Y. Hwang, Brian J. Matz, and Augustine Casiday (Washington, DC: Catholic University of America Press, 2014), p. 4.

On Pelagius' emphasis on the goodness of creation and freedom, see *CG*, p. 159.

On the attraction of Pelagius' teaching, see *AH*, p. 347; see the same work, p. 343, on Pelagius' rejection of original sin and of the need for grace.

On the beginning of the controversy with Caelistius, see *AT*, p. 319; and *AH*, pp. 344–345.

On Cyprian's view of original sin and its prevalence in North Africa, see TeSelle, pp. 1–2.

On the Pelagian view of grace as an external divine help, see *CG*, p. 159; and *AT*, p. 320.

St. Augustine's Response to Pelagian Teaching

On Augustine's initial involvement in the Pelagian controversy, see *AT*, p. 319.

On Augustine's view of Pelagius, see *AH*, pp. 345, 357; and *AT*, p. 320.

On the universal horizon of Augustine's teaching, see *AH*, p. 351.

On Augustine's teaching on original sin, see Mathijs Lamberigts, "Original Sin," in *The Oxford Guide to the Historical Reception of Augustine* (Oxford University Press, online ed., 2013).

On man's inability to overcome the state of sin by his effort, see *AT*, p. 319; on the absolute need for grace, see *GC*, pp. 36–37.

On the distinction between the desire for good and accomplishing the good, see M. Huftier, "Libre arbitre, liberté et péché chez saint Augustin," in *Recherches de Théologie Ancienne et Médiévale* 33 (July–December 1966), pp. 195–196.

On infant baptism as a sign of the gratuitousness of grace, see *CG*, p. 164; this work cites W. Harmless, "Baptism," in J. C. Cavadini and A. D. Fitzgerald, eds., *Augustine through the Ages: An Encyclopedia* (Grand Rapids: William B. Eerdmans, 1999), pp. 84–91.

On *delectatio victrix*, see *GC*, p. 37; and *CG*, p. 166.

"what at one time": Augustine, *The Confessions*, trans. J. G. Pilkington, *Nicene and Post-Nicene Fathers*, series 1, vol. 1, ed. Philip Schaff (Buffalo: Christian Literature Publishing Co., 1887; online ed. at New Advent, ed. Kevin Knight), bk. 9, chap. 1.

On the need for actual grace, see *CG*, p. 165.

On the different contexts for the Manichean and Pelagian controversies, see Huftier, "Libre arbitre," p. 280.

On the interaction of grace and freedom in Augustine, see M. Huftier, "Libre arbitre," pp. 196, 198–199.

"invites or draws": TeSelle, p. 13.

The Church's Teaching on the Need for Grace

On the North African bishops' opposition to Pelagianism, see Paul A. Taylor, "St. Augustine: The Doctor of Grace," in *Life of the Spirit* 5, no. 50 (August 1950), p. 74.

On Pope Zosimus' condemnation and its background, see *AH*, pp. 361–363.

On the lack of "middle ground" in Pelagianism, see TeSelle, p. 5.

Regarding Pelagius' position on infant baptism, see K. Stasiak, "Baptism of Infants," in *NCE*, vol. 7, p. 69.

The text of the Canons of the Council of Carthage (418) on sin and grace are in *The Code of Canons of the African Church*, trans. Henry Percival, *Nicene and Post-Nicene Fathers*, series 2, vol. 14, ed. Philip Schaff and Henry Wace (Peabody, MA: Hendrickson, 1995; reprint of original by Scribner, 1900); text of the Canons for the Fifteenth Council begin with canon 109, p. 496.

On the reasoning behind Augustine's notion of original sin, see Lamberigts.

On Pelagianism and its core assertion of freedom, see S. J. McKenna, "Pelagius and Pelagianism," in *NCE*, vol. 11, p. 62.

"inspires us": Canon 112, in *The Code of Canons of the African Church*.

On Pelagius' notion of illumination, see Joseph Pohle, "Pelagius and Pelagianism," *The Catholic Encyclopedia*, vol. 11 (New York: Robert Appleton Company, 1911; online ed. at New Advent, ed. Kevin Knight); see also G. F. Wiggers, *An Historical Presentation of Augustinism and Pelagianism from the Original Sources* (New York: Gould, Newman, and Saxton, 1840, pp. 185–186.

"thinking that" and "it is fatal": John Paul II, Apostolic Letter on the Close of the Great Jubilee Year 2000 *Novo Millennio Ineunte* (January 6, 2001), no. 38, Vatican website: www.vatican.va.

Chapter 8: God's Grace and the Reality of Human Freedom

Man's Freedom before the Reality of Sin

Regarding Aquinas' teaching on the disorder caused by sin, see *ST* 1-2.85.1.

On Aquinas' recognition of man's freedom after original sin, see *ST* 1-2.102.2., as well as commentary in *AT*, p. 348.

"cannot harm": Council of Trent, *Decree on Original Sin*, no. 5.

On sufficient grace, see *CG*, p. 200; and "Sufficient Grace," in *NCE*, vol. 6, p. 409.

Regarding efficacious grace, see *AT*, p. 494; on the scriptural basis of this topic, and *gratia invicta*, see *CG*, pp. 200–201.

Regarding Lorda's position on resisting grace and the value of the terms *sufficient* and *efficient*, see *AT*, p. 494.

The Thought of Baius and Jansen Regarding Freedom and Grace

On the context of Baius, see *AT*, p. 349; and *CG*, p. 205.

On the thought of Baius, see P. J. Donnelly, "Baius and Baianism," in *NCE*, vol. 2, pp. 18–21; and *CG*, pp. 205–206.

"motion of the soul": Baius, *De charitate*, chap. 2, cited in Donnelly, p. 20.

On the background to Jansen, see "Jansen, Cornelius Otto (Jansenius)," in *NCE*, vol. 7, p. 714.

On Jansenism, see *CG*, pp. 207–209; Jacques M. Gres-Gayer, "Jansenism," in *NCE*, vol. 7, pp. 715, 720; and *AT*, p. 350.

On the historical spread of Jansenism, see Jacques M. Gres-Gayer, "Jansenism," in *Europe, 1450–1789: Encyclopedia of the Early Modern World*, vol. 3, ed. Jonathan Dewald (New York: Scribner, 2004; online ed. at Gale ebooks), p. 338.

This analysis of Jansenism draws also from Ronald Knox, "Jansenism: Its Genius," in *Enthusiasm: A Chapter in the History of Religion* (Notre Dame, IN: University of Notre Dame Press, 1994), pp. 209–212.

The De Auxiliis Controversy

Regarding Molina's position, see Mark B. Wiebe, *On Evil, Providence, and Freedom: A New Reading of Molina* (DeKalb, IL: Northern Illinois University Press, 2017), pp. 9–10; see also *CG*, p. 203.

Regarding Aquinas' thought concerning primary and secondary causes, see *AT*, p. 496, which makes reference to Aquinas' *Summa Contra Gentiles*, bk. 3, chap. 148, and *ST* 1-2.6.1. and 10.4.

On the problem posed by God's providence and freedom, see Wiebe, p. 81.

On *scientia media*, see *CG*, p. 203; and F. L. Sheerin, "Molinism," in *NCE*, vol. 9, p. 771.

On the position of Báñez, see W. J. Hill, "Báñez and Bañezianism," in *NCE*, vol. 2, p. 50.

On the harmony between freedom and grace in this position, see *EG*, p. 294; and *AT*, p. 497.

On the background regarding the *de auxiliis* congregation, see T. Ryan, "Congregatio de Auxiliis," in *NCE*, vol. 4, pp. 111–113.

"Freedom finds": Escrivá, *Friends of God*, no. 27.

Grace, Good Works, and Merit

"does not lessen": John Paul II, Encyclical Letter on the Splendor of Truth *Veritatis Splendor* (August 6, 1993), no. 24, Vatican website: www.vatican.va.

Regarding the scriptural basis for merit, see C. S. Sullivan, "Merit," in *NCE*, vol. 9, p. 510.

On man not having any merit, strictly speaking, see *ST* 1-2.114.1.

On the "right" to eternal life through grace, see *ST* 1-2.114.2.

"is adopted": *ST* 1-2.114.3.; Scripture quotation is from this text.

On condign and congruent merit, see *ST* 1-2.114.3, 8; see also *CG*, no. 351.

On God's decree to grant an increase in grace for man's response, see *DJ*, chap. 10.

On congruent merit and for historical background on merit, see Alister E. McGrath, Iustitia Dei: *A History of the Christian Doctrine of Justification*, 4th ed. (Cambridge, UK: Cambridge University Press, 2020), pp. 156–163.

On the Church's teaching that we can merit graces for ourselves and for others: see *CCC*, no. 2010.

On Luther's rejection of merit, see *AT*, p. 500.

On the Church's teaching that merit does not belong to us except by God's freely given grace: see *CCC*, no. 2007–2008.

On Augustine's teaching regarding merit, see Sullivan, "Merit," p. 511; citation of Augustine is from *Sermones*, 170.10.10, in Jacques-Paul Migne, ed. *Patrologiae Cursus Completus, Series Latina* (Paris: J.-P. Migne, 1844–1865; online edition by Chadwyck-Healey, Inc.), 38:932, https://www.proquest.com/patrologialatina/advanced.

Regarding the teaching of the Council of Trent: The Council recalls Augustine when it says, "He wishes the things that are His gifts to be their merits," in *DJ*, chap. 16; on justification as fruit of Christ and his passion, see *DJ*, chaps. 7 and 16.

"always precedes": *DJ*, chap. 16.

On the possibility of merit for an increase in grace, see *DJ*, canon 32.

"The grace of Christ": see *CCC*, no. 1742.

On grace seeking a free response, see *CG*, p. 357.

On God and man as totally involved in the salvific action, see *EG*, p. 287.

"By the working": see *CCC*, no. 1742.

Chapter 9: Grace, Freedom, and God's Plan of Salvation

The Semi-Pelagian Controversy: The Debate on the Beginning of Faith and Predestination

Regarding Augustine's affirmations during the Pelagian controversy, see *DG*, p. 5.

On the circumstances behind the controversy at Hadrumetum, see *DG*, p. 8.

Regarding the position of the monks, see Augustine, *A Treatise on Grace and Free Will*, in *Augustine: Anti-Pelagian Writings, Nicene and Post-Nicene Fathers*, series 1, vol. 5, ed. Philip Schaff (Peabody, MA: Hendrickson, 1995; reprint of Christian Literature Publishing Co., 1887), chap. 1; see also Volker Henning Drecoll, "*De correptione et gratia*," in *The Oxford Guide to the Historical Reception of Augustine*, ed. Karla Pollmann and Willemien Otten (Oxford: Oxford University Press, online ed., 2014); see also *AH*, p. 402.

The two treatises in response to the Hadrumetum are *A Treatise on Grace and Free Will* and *A Treatise on Rebuke and Grace*, both in *Nicene and Post-Nicene Fathers*, vol. 5.

For commentary on Augustine's position on the Word of God's recognition of freedom, see *DG*, p. 17; for his position on the will's need for grace to carry out God's law, see *DG*, p. 18.

Apropos of the cases where God is said to harden the heart, see Augustine, *Treatise on Grace and Free Will*, chap. 42.

On Augustine's teaching on predestination in response to the Semi-Pelagians, see S. J. McKenna, "Semi-Pelagianism," in *NCE*, vol. 12, p. 899.

On justification as based purely on a free choice of God and allusion to Rom 8:29, see Augustine, *A Treatise on Rebuke and Grace*, chap. 14.

On the change in Augustine's position regarding man's capacity to desire the good without grace, see Boniface Ramsey, "John Cassian and Augustine," in *Grace for Grace*, pp. 128–129; the footnote on p. 128 contains the quote "God's grace conquered," which comes from *Retractions*, 2.1.3.

On Augustine's increasing insistence on the gratuity of grace and grace as reward for grace, see *DG*, p. 19, which comments on *A Treatise on Grace and Free Will*.

On Augustine's attempt to reconcile the priority of grace with freedom, see *AH*, p. 406.

On God's grace as an essential element for good, see *DG*, p. 20.

On the spread of controversy to Gaul and opposition there, see *DG*, pp. 40, 52, as well as *AH*, p. 403; *DG* 52 quotes Letter 226 of Augustine on the Semi-Pelagian view of "some beginning" in the will.

On the two final works of Augustine, see *AH*, p. 409.

On the shift in Augustine's position to exclude any human element before grace, see *DG*, p. 51.

Allusion to "at the present time" is found in Augustine, *On the Predestination of the Saints*, chap. 7, in *Nicene and Post-Nicene Fathers*, series 1, vol. 5; Scripture text is from the RSV.

On perseverance as gift, see Augustine, *On the Gift of Perseverance*, chap. 9, in *Nicene and Post-Nicene Fathers*, series 1, vol. 5.

On Augustine's awareness of how committed Christians could turn away, and the need for a stable foundation in God, see *AH*, pp. 407–408.

On Augustine's realization that the free choice of God is source of faithfulness, see his work *On Rebuke and Grace*, chap. 16.

On perseverance as a gift that cannot be taken away, see Augustine, *Gift of Perseverance*, chap. 12.

On the continued opposition after his final works, see McKenna, "Semi-Pelagianism," p. 899.

"I confess" and "judgments are": Augustine, *Gift of Perseverance*, chap. 18.

On Christians as chosen in advance and the harmony of this with freedom, see Augustine, *Gift of Perseverance*, chaps. 50–51.

"not in himself": Augustine, *Gift of Perseverance*, chap. 51.

On mutual misunderstanding in Semi-Pelagian controversy, see *DG*, p. 128.

On the misrepresentation of Augustine's position and the adjustment of his position, see *DG*, pp. 134–138.

On the differences of perspective in the Semi-Pelagian controversy, see *AT*, p. 472.

On the interaction of grace and free will in the teaching of Cassian and Faustus, see *DG*, p. 165.

The Second Council of Orange and the Resolution of the Semi-Pelagian Controversy

On the roots of the position of monks who opposed Augustine's notion of grace, and Cassian's vision of this notion as a threat, see *DG*, pp. 72, 80.

On the tendency of Greek Fathers to speak about exercise of the will without mention of grace, see Ramsey, "John Cassian and Augustine," p. 126.

On Caesarius' Augustinian background, see *DG*, p. 208; regarding Caesarius' emphasis on repentance and good works, see *DG*, pp. 216–217.

See *DG*, pp. 220–221, apropos of Caesarius' teaching on human action and freedom as based in grace.

On Caesarius' adjustment of Augustine's teaching, see *DG*, pp. 222–223.

On Caesarius' teaching on prevenient grace, see C. M. Aherne, "Orange, Councils of," in *NCE*, vol. 10, p. 620.

On background to the Council of Orange, see McKenna, "Semi-Pelagianism," p. 900.

Text of the Canons of the Second Council of Orange provided by The Catholic Resource Network, Internet History Sourcebooks Project, Fordham University, https://sourcebooks.fordham.edu/basis/orange.txt.

"ability and responsibility": from "Conclusion" of Canons of the Second Council of Orange.

On this Council's rejection of a predestination to evil, see also "Conclusion" of the Canons.

For commentary on the Council's stance on predestination, see *DG*, pp. 231–232.

Predestination and God's Will for All to Be Saved

On the original sense of Augustine's teaching of predestination, see *CG*, pp. 167–169; with specific regard to condemnation, see *AT*, p. 474.

On double predestination, see *AT*, p. 475.

On Gottschalk's position, see *CG*, p. 173.

On the significance of the Council of Quiercy's teaching, see *AT*, p. 475.

On the teaching of the Protestant reformers with regard to predestination, see A. G. Palladino, "Predestination (In Non-Catholic Theology)," in *NCE*, vol. 11, p. 654; on the theological atmosphere of the time, see *AT*, p. 476.

Regarding Luther's view on predestination and Lutheran doctrine on this point, see Palladino, pp. 654–655.

On Calvin's notion of double predestination as a consequence of his view of God and man, and the details of his view, see R. Matzerath and P. Soergel, "Calvinism," in *NCE*, vol. 2, p. 893.

On Calvin's view of freedom, see Palladino, p. 655.

"predisposing grace": *DJ*, chap. 5.

For the Council of Trent's rejection of predestination to evil, see *DJ*, canon 17; for the Council's affirmation of the justified man's freedom to turn from God, see *DJ*, canon 12.

On the Council of Trent's reluctance to offer an authoritative statement on predestination, see McGrath, p. 336; see n. 134 on the same page for how predestination is always to salvation.

On the European settlement of the Americas as a moment for reflection on how grace operates, see M. Eminyan, "Salvation, Necessity of the Church for," in *NCE*, vol. 12, p. 624.

On invincible ignorance, see J. B. Nugent and F. D. Nealy, "Ignorance," in *NCE*, vol. 7, p. 314.

For Aquinas' teaching on the first moral option, see *ST* 1-2.89.6; see also commentary in *AT*, p. 480.

On the distinction between the ordinary and extraordinary paths of grace, see *AT*, p. 477.

"while having": John Paul II, Encyclical Letter on the Permanent Validity of the Church's Missionary Mandate *Redemptoris Missio* (December 7, 1990), no. 10, Vatican website: www.vatican.va.

"truth and grace to all": *LG*, no. 8.

"the truth definitively revealed by the Lord" and "the necessity of conversion to Jesus Christ": Congregation for the Doctrine of the Faith, Declaration on the Unicity and Salvific Universality of Jesus Christ and the Church *Dominus Iesus* (August 6, 2000), no. 22, Vatican website: www.vatican.va.

Chapter 10: The Progress and Final End of the Life of Grace

The Baptismal Gift of Divine Filiation and Its Meaning

For Illanes' affirmation of the love of God poured out upon man, see *TE*, p. 207.

On the pre-Christian notion of virtue, see *CG*, pp. 304–305 and *AT*, p. 508.

"nothing else": *The Book of Her Life*, in *The Collected Works of St. Teresa of Avila*, trans. Kieran Kavanaugh and Otilio Rodriguez, 2nd rev. ed. (Washington, DC: ICS, 1987), chap. 8, no. 5.

Josemaría Escrivá describes the "sense" of divine filiation in a letter of January 25, 1961, no. 52, cited in Ernst Burkhart and Javier López, *Ordinary Life and Holiness in the Teaching of St. Josemaría: A Study in Spiritual Theology*, trans. Javier del Castillo, vol. 2 (New York: Scepter, 2020; original Spanish ed., Madrid: Rialp, 2011), p. 89.

On experiencing God's fatherhood in thoughts, desires, and affections, see Escrivá, *Friends of God*, no. 146.

On the *Catechism*'s teaching that the Lord's Prayer to the Father takes place together with the Son and Holy Spirit: see *CCC*, no. 2789.

Identification with Christ as Goal of the Spiritual Life

On the centrality of identification with Christ in the spiritual tradition, see *AT*, pp. 402–406.

On grace as the life of Christ in the believer, see *CG*, p. 356.

On Christ who reveals God in his human nature, see *TE*, p. 222.

"worked with human": *GS*, p. 22.

"external model": Fernando Ocáriz, Pastoral Visit to Barcelona, Spain (July 26, 2021), quoted in "In Milan: 'First Comes Our Relationship with Christ and Concern for Others,'" Opus Dei, August 10, 2021, https://opusdei.org/en/article/monsignor-fernando-ocariz-in-barcelona-a-smile-on-the-face-brings-joy-to-the-soul/.

"dynamic principle": *TE*, p. 246. On the connection between identification and personal union with Christ, see *TE*, p. 231.

"The sanctity": Alphonsus Liguori, *The Practice of the Love of Jesus Christ*, trans. Peter Heinegg (Liguori, MO: Liguori Publications, 1997), 1.

The Holy Spirit in the Life of the Christian

"the Lord, the giver": text of Nicene Creed is found in *CCC*, part 1, section 1, chap. 3, art. 2.

For Basil on the command of Mt 28:19, see *On the Holy Spirit*, chap.10, no. 24, *Nicene and Post-Nicene Fathers,* series 2, vol. 8, ed. Philip Schaff and Henry Wace (Peabody, MA: Hendrickson, 1995; reprint of Christian Literature Publishing Co., 1895); "to every" is from the same work, chap. 11, no. 27.

"Now you feel": Josemaría Escrivá, *The Forge* (New York: Scepter, 1987), no. 430.

On the meaning of docility to the Holy Spirit, see *TE*, p. 264.

"Through thee": Hymn "Veni Creator," Divine Office of Pentecost Sunday, in *Handbook of Prayers*, ed. James Socias, 6th American ed. (Woodridge, IL: Midwest Theological Forum, 2007), p. 428.

On the Christian's search for God in human realities, see *TE*, pp. 322–324.

The Blessed Virgin Mary as Model and Mediatrix for the Christian

On translation of Lk 1:28 as "crowned with favor," see Augustin George, "Mary," trans. Henry J. Bourguignon, in *DBT*, p. 339.

On the understanding of *kecharitomene* in Catholic theology, see Bastero, p. 106.

Regarding John Paul II's teaching on the fullness of grace given to all Christians and Mary, and "in a special": Encyclical Letter On the Blessed Virgin Mary in the Life of the Pilgrim Church *Redemptoris Mater* (March 25, 1987), no. 8, Vatican website: www.vatican.va.

"cooperated by": *LG*, no. 61.

"the Church has": *LG*, no. 65.

On Mary as mediatrix, see *LG*, no. 62.

The Progress and Culmination of the Spiritual Life

"act habitually": see *CCC*, no. 2752.

"grace received": *CG*, no. 356.

On growth in grace as gift and not merit, see Joseph P. Wawrykow, *God's Grace and Human Action: 'Merit' in the Theology of Thomas Aquinas* (Notre Dame, IN: University of Notre Dame Press, 1995), p. 250.

On God's granting an increase in grace in response to man's cooperation, see *CG*, p. 351.

On the Church as sign and means of salvation, see *LG*, no. 1.

On progress in grace, see *EG*, pp. 209–211; on progress in grace and in virtue, see Wawrykow, pp. 171, 224, 227.

Regarding lukewarmness, see *TE*, pp. 409–411.

On the traditional three stages of spiritual progress in Aquinas, see *TE*, p. 561, and more broadly in the spiritual tradition, *TE*, pp. 563–564.

On the need to avoid seeing the stages too rigidly and on the uniqueness of each individual, see *TE*, pp. 565–566.

On the residual tendency to sin which remains within man, see *ST* 1-2.109.9; and Wawrykow, pp. 171, 227.

On grace as a seed, see ST 1-2.114.3.

"the sons of God" and "will answer": *GS*, no. 39.

Acknowledgments

I would like to express my sincere thanks to Robert Singerline, Meredith Koopman, and the entire Scepter team. I'm also very grateful to those who have reviewed and offered suggestions, especially Larry Olsen and Fr. Henry Bocala. My hope is that this work might offer an opportunity for many persons to reflect more deeply on the Church's rich teaching on grace, a theme so familiar and yet at the same time so intensely debated over the centuries. The current moment, in which we commemorate sixty years since the Second Vatican Council, offers an apt moment to explore this theme in line with the teaching of the Council, "the great grace bestowed on the Church in the twentieth century" and "a sure compass by which to take our bearings" in the twenty-first century (John Paul II, *Novo Millennio Ineunte*, n. 57).